Goal Analysis

How to clarify your goals so you can actually achieve them

Third Edition

Robert F. Mager

Books by Robert F. Mager

Preparing Instructional Objectives, *Third Edition**

Measuring Instructional Results, *Third Edition**

Analyzing Performance Problems, *Third Edition**
(with Peter Pipe)

Goal Analysis, *Third Edition**

How to Turn Learners On . . . without turning them off, *Third Edition**

Making Instruction Work, *Second Edition**

Developing Vocational Instruction (with Kenneth Beach)

Troubleshooting the Troubleshooting Course

The How to Write a Book Book

What Every Manager Should Know About Training

*Sold as a six-volume set (The Mager Six-Pack)

About CEP

CEP helps organizations profit from planned changes such as mergers, acquisitions, re-structuring, globalization and ERP implementations. Using Dr. Robert F. Mager's renowned research-based methodology, our consultants help clients avoid the workforce performance problems that are likely to prevent them from achieving the results they expect from implementing strategic change.

We have the strategies, training, tools and resources to make your workforce a true competitive advantage.

Workforce Performance...**WE WROTE THE BOOK.**

For more information, contact:
The Center for Effective Performance, Inc.
1100 Johnson Ferry Rd., Suite 150
Atlanta, GA 30342
(770) 458-4080 or (800) 558-4237
www.cepworldwide.com

ISBN 1-879-618-04-4 (PREVIOUSLY ISBN 1-56103-339-1)
ISBN 1-879-618-15-X (SIX-VOLUME SET)
Library of Congress Catalog Card Number: 96-72445
Printed in the United States of America

10 11 12   12 11 10 9 8 7

Contents

Preface

Once upon a time in the land of Fuzz, King Aling called in his cousin Ding and commanded, "Go ye out into all of Fuzzland and find me the goodest of men, whom I shall reward for his goodness."

"But how will I know one when I see one?" asked the Fuzzy.

"Why, he will be *sincere*," scoffed the king, and whacked off a leg for his impertinence.

So, the Fuzzy limped out to find a good man. But soon he returned confused and empty-handed.

"But how will I know one when I see one?" he asked again.

"Why, he will be *dedicated*," grumbled the king and whacked off another leg for his impertinence.

So the Fuzzy hobbled away once more to look for the goodest of men. But again he returned, confused and empty-handed.

"But how will I know one when I see one?" he pleaded.

"Why, he will have *an empathetic understanding of his self-actualizing potential*," fumed the king and whacked off another leg for his impertinence.

So the Fuzzy, now on his last leg, hopped out to continue his search. In time, he returned with the wisest, most sincere and dedicated Fuzzy in all of Fuzzland and stood him before the king.

"Why, this man won't do at all," roared the king. "He is much too thin to suit me." Whereupon, he whacked off the last leg of the Fuzzy, who fell to the floor with a squishy thump.

The moral of this fable is that . . . *if you can't tell one when you see one, you may wind up without a leg to stand on.*

IF YOU CAN'T TELL ONE WHEN YOU SEE ONE, YOU MAY WIND UP WITHOUT A LEG TO STAND ON.

If your goals—your visions—are important to achieve, then it is essential that you do more than just talk about them in "Fuzzy" terms. And that is just as true for organizational and community goals as it is for personal and family goals. Broad statements of intent can be achieved only to the degree that their meaning is understood, to the degree that you can recognize achievement of the goals when you see it.

And that is what *Goal Analysis* is about. The goal analysis procedure can be very useful in helping you to describe the *meaning* of goals and visions you hope to achieve, whether those goals deal with attitude, appreciation, understanding, success, or profitability. It is a procedure designed to help you determine the important dimensions or components of a goal, so that you will be able to make good decisions about how to accomplish the goal and about how to keep track of your progress toward goal achievement. It is a procedure that anyone will find useful, from techies to homemakers, from students to managers, and will even be useful to those who feel that their jobs are unlike any others and very hard to describe.

It is *not* the object of this book to tell you what to achieve or what you should mean by the words you use. But if you have ever wished that you or the organization with which you are affiliated could be better at accomplishing their goals, *Goal Analysis* will give you the tools you need.

Robert F. Mager

Carefree, Arizona
January 1997

1

What It's All About

Almost everyone wants to be more successful. Regardless of who they are or what they do, individuals want to be knowledgeable, have poise, be able to communicate and listen, and a thousand other things. Organizations want to shape their vision, and they want their employees to provide good customer service, achieve high morale, conserve energy, be responsible, appreciate diversity, and a thousand other things. Members of the clergy want to increase reverence, encourage unselfish devotion, provide merciful ministry, and a thousand other things.

Almost all people want to improve these things either in themselves or in others. "They need to have a better attitude" and "We've got to teach them to be properly motivated" are commonly heard expressions. "We need to improve their self-concept" and "We want them to behave in a professional manner" are others. The uttering of these important intentions, however, is only a beginning step toward their accomplishment. Saying them isn't the same as achieving them.

What to do? What steps should we take to accomplish the many important goals (visions) in our lives? Should we tell people what to do? Should we organize a course and have them attend? Should we establish rules, invent forms, punish offenders, praise the good? The key question is "Exactly what should we do to accomplish our important goals?"

The answer is "There is no way to decide what action to take until we know what we are trying to accomplish." Too often, people would rather do something than think about the purpose of the doing. For them, action is the same as progress.

And when it comes to goal achievement, that action all too frequently takes the form of instruction. "We've got to teach them to have the right attitude," they say. But "attitude" isn't a skill that requires know-how. So what is there to teach? Or "We've got to teach them to improve their citizenship." Again, there's no clue as to what, if anything, needs to be taught.

If there is a real difference between what people can do and what they need to be able to do, and if those people have a genuine need to do what they can't do, then instruction may help. Maybe. But maybe a different action is called for. There's no way to know until the intended outcome is clearly stated. Consider this nutty dialogue between a hypothetical doctor and woman:

Doc: Ah, good morning, madam.

Mad: Good morning, doctor.

Doc: Just a moment and I'll have your prescription all written out.

Mad: Wait a minute. . .

Doc: No time like the present, you know.

Mad: But I haven't even told you why I'm here yet.

Doc: No need. I've been a doctor for seventeen years.

Mad: Don't you even *examine* people?

Doc: What for? I've been trained and licensed to practice, and I know what most people need in the way of treatment.

Mad: You give everybody the same treatment?

Doc: Of course. Saves time.

Mad: That's crazy!

Doc: Not at all. Most patients improve. Some improve more than others, of course, but that's mostly because they try harder.

Mad: What about the ones who get worse?

Doc: No problem. I label them as failures and send them on . . . and on . . . and on. Ah, by the way, why are you here?

Mad: I was the new receptionist. And good-bye!

You see the point. Action is easy. What isn't so easy is relating actions to outcomes. What isn't easy is *purposeful* activity, activity that will get you where you want to go. And if instruction (or any other remedy) is to be successful, there must be a connection between the problem and the solution, between the need for the instruction and the nature of the instruction. Often the connection is obvious. If you want to be able to play the piano, the instruction needs to provide skills and practice in playing the piano. If you want to be able to make a speech, you need to practice speechmaking.

Sometimes, however, the connection between the intention—that is, the intended result—and the actions needed to get the result isn't so clear. Consider this dialogue between a professor and student:

Stud: I refuse to pay you for this course.

Prof: Why? Didn't I teach you how to make the finest buggy whips ever created?

Stud: Yes, you did.

Prof: Well then?

Stud: But I took this course because I wanted to understand history.

Prof: Can you deny that buggy whips were used by some of the most important people in history?

Stud: I suppose not.

Prof: Can you deny that buggy whips are an integral part of history?

Stud: I don't know. I never learned any history. I only learned how to make buggy whips.

Prof: But wasn't I successful in teaching you how to make good buggy whips?

Stud: Yes. But the fact remains . . .

Prof: Yes?

Stud: You didn't solve my problem.

It seems pretty obvious that if your goal is to improve students' understanding of history, you don't proceed to make them expert buggy-whip makers. Nor would you instruct them in welding or weaving. But what *would* you do? Maybe instructing isn't even the right approach. Maybe some other action is indicated. Or maybe *no* action at all. How can you decide how to proceed *until* you know what "understanding history" means?

To take other examples, how should you proceed if the goal is to make "better citizens"? What should you do if the goal is to achieve "good judgment," "perceptive listening," "motivated workers," or "effective therapists"? Though these states may be among the most important to achieve—and all goals *sound* important—*the act of stating them in the abstract does little to suggest the means of their achievement.*

Shapes and Sizes

Goal statements come in all sorts of shapes and sizes and are wrapped in all sorts of words. Some are stated briefly; others are not. One thing they have in common is that they all sound important.

Some goals refer to us as individuals:
- be a good citizen
- have self-confidence
- be a knowledgeable consumer

Others refer to the organization:
- be technologically innovative
- offer an enlightened workplace
- provide opportunities for personal growth

Still others refer to the environment or the community:
- enhance urban livability
- provide a modern environment
- maintain empathetic public servants

But if a goal is important to achieve, then it is important to do more about that achievement than to simply talk about it in abstract terms. Again, that's just where goal analysis comes in.* (It will help show you just what steps to take to accomplish your goals.)

The Goal of this Book

The goal of this book is to help you "know when and how to do a goal analysis." But that's a fuzzy. It sounds nice, but it doesn't tell you what "know" means. It sort of points in the direction of

*In technical jargon, the goal analysis procedure is called "developing an operational definition."

the desired outcomes, but it doesn't describe them very well.

Aha! This is just the situation that calls for a goal analysis. Having performed one on this very fuzzy statement, I can now be more specific in telling you what the goal of this book means.

The goal, "know when and how to do a goal analysis," means:

1. Be able to tell the difference between statements that describe abstractions and those that describe performances.

2. Having identified a goal that you consider important to achieve, be able to describe the performances that represent your meaning of the goal. In other words, be able to describe specific outcomes that, if achieved, will cause you to agree that the goal is also achieved.

As a test of your success with the procedure, you would select a goal you think important, carry out the procedure, and then answer the question, "If a person exhibited the performances I have described in a way I have described, would I agree that he or she has achieved (represents) my goal?" When you are able to answer "yes," you will be finished with the analysis. If your answer is "no," further analysis would be indicated.

What Next?

The goal analysis procedure is not a procedure that you set out to do because you *want* to; rather, it's something that you do because you *have* to. Let's take a look at the bigger picture to see just where the goal analysis procedure fits in.

2
When To Do It

Where does the goal analysis fit into the larger scheme of things? To answer that, we'll need to take a brief look at the bigger picture, which relates to our intent to improve something.

Executives and managers work to improve the functioning of their organizations; trainers work to improve the ability of their trainees to perform their jobs; teachers want to better prepare their students to cope successfully in the world around them; and parents want to help their children become productive, responsible, and happy adults. And, as individuals, our intent is often to improve some aspect of our lives (e.g., adopt more useful habits) or to strengthen our skills.

There are a number of procedures available through which to accomplish these improvements, and here are very brief descriptions of some of the main ones.

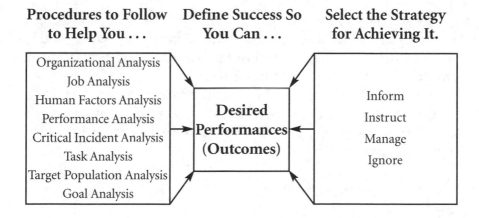

Procedures to Follow to Help You ...	Define Success So You Can ...	Select the Strategy for Achieving It.
Organizational Analysis Job Analysis Human Factors Analysis Performance Analysis Critical Incident Analysis Task Analysis Target Population Analysis Goal Analysis	Desired Performances (Outcomes)	Inform Instruct Manage Ignore

Organizational Analysis

An organizational analysis is used to determine just what it is the organization should look like to best accomplish its mission. The focus is on (1) verifying that the various components of the organization (division, departments, sections, etc.) are designed and connected in the best possible way to get the organization where it wants to go and (2) specifying meaningful outcomes that will lead to mission accomplishment. An organizational analysis also looks at all the supports (e.g., policies, equipment, trained people, etc.) that need to be in place to ensure that people can do their jobs effectively.

Job Analysis

A *job* consists of a collection of tasks. Sometimes this is a fixed collection of tasks that can be carefully described, and sometimes the boundaries of the job are intended to be flexible (e.g., "Your job title is Corporate Troubleshooter, and your job is to do what you think needs to be done"). A *job analysis* is intended to identify the tasks that should define a job, to name and describe the tasks that will best serve the organization (as defined by the organizational analysis) in producing the desired accomplishments (outcomes).

Human Factors Analysis

These analyses are intended to find out how best to design equipment so that it will fit the human beings expected to use it. The purpose is to find out how to make the equipment "user friendly," easy to use, and idiot-proof.

For example, a great deal of human factors analysis is done in the design of aircraft cockpits, not so much to make them comfortable for the pilots, but to make information instantly available to them when they need it.

Whatever the specific intent, the general intent is to find ways to improve human performance.

Performance Analysis

The performance analysis is used to determine why people aren't doing something they are supposed to be doing or why they are doing something they shouldn't be doing. It helps one to select solutions that will eliminate a performance discrepancy (the difference between what is happening and what should be happening). The analysis consists of evaluating the size or importance of a performance discrepancy, then determining whether the discrepancy exists because of a lack of skill or motivation to perform a known skill or because of obstacles that prevent the desired performance from occurring.

Critical Incident Analysis

This procedure (sometimes called a *significant incident analysis*) attempts to answer the question, "What isn't happening according to expectation?" By collecting and analyzing incidents of deviations from the expected (accidents, for example), it is possible to determine what actions might be taken to remedy (reduce or eliminate) the incidents. Sometimes the remedy is information, sometimes it is instruction, and sometimes it involves actions such as color-coding equipment or clarifying directions.

Task Analysis

If the performance analysis indicates that people don't know *how* to do what they need to be able to do, instruction is usually, but not always, needed as a remedy. When instruction appears to be a solution, the next question to be answered is "What should the instruction accomplish?" The task analysis is one way to derive the answer to this question. This technique reveals the components of competent performance—that is, it provides a step-by-step look at how competent people perform a task, so that decisions can more easily be made about what *other* people would have to learn if *they* are to perform in the same competent manner.

Target Population Analysis

An act that is wasteful of human motivation, as well as of time and money, is that of "teaching" people things they already know. The target population analysis helps to eliminate this problem. This technique consists of a careful examination of the characteristics (abilities, education, interests, biases, experience) of those for whom instruction is intended. With this information available, it is possible to select instruction for any individual by subtracting what the individual already knows from what the individual needs to know. The remainder can then be prescribed as the curriculum for that individual.

The information revealed by the target population analysis is also useful in adjusting the examples, the language, the media mix through which the instruction and practice are presented, and the speed of the instruction, so that they more closely match the needs of the people for whom the instruction is intended.

Goal Analysis

People are often expected to perform in ways that are not reflected in tasks. In addition to performing certain skills, they are expected to "appreciate music," "show respect for school," "develop a proper customer attitude," or "take pride in their work." Since it isn't possible to watch them developing or appreciating, and if these states are important for them to achieve, how will you proceed? How will you decide *if* instruction will help them to achieve the desired state? And if it will, how will you decide *what kind* of instruction to organize?

A task analysis won't help, because there is no task to observe. A critical incident analysis won't help, because there are no errors or problems to tabulate. A target population analysis is useful mainly as a procedure for adjusting existing instructional objectives, so that is out. Likewise, a performance analysis can't be carried out until the relevant performances are identified.

This is where goal analysis fits. The function of goal analysis is to define the indefinable, to tangibilitate the intangible— to help you say what you mean by your important but abstract goals (or *fuzzies,* as they will be called in this book). *With this procedure, it is possible to describe the essential elements of abstract states—to identify the main performances that constitute the meaning of the goal.* Once you know the performances that collectively define the goal, you will be in a better position to decide which of these performances need to be taught and which need to be managed. Then you can select the most appropriate teaching or management procedures and arrange to measure your progress toward success.

We Use It All the Time

Carpenters may set out to lay a floor and suddenly discover a need to use their tape measure. They may set out to set a window and again have to reach for their tape measure. As a matter of fact, no matter which task they begin, it is likely that they will need to use their tape measure somewhere during completion of the task.

The same is true of goal analysis. While you may sometimes deliberately set out to complete a goal analysis, there are many other instances in which you will discover that you need to complete a goal analysis if you want to get on with the task you are performing.

For example:

**When you're engaging in:**	_**Do a goal analysis when you hear:**_
Organizational Analysis	_"The organization needs to be more flexible and resilient."_
Job Analysis	_"They need to be self-starters."_
Human Factors Analysis	_"This gismo needs to be 'user friendly'."_
Performance Analysis	_"They should be more safety conscious."_
Critical Incident Analysis	_"There are too many accidents."_
Task Analysis	_"The next step is to answer the phone in a friendly manner."_
Target Population Analysis	_"They are highly motivated."_

In each of the instances above, and in thousands like them, a goal analysis would be appropriate, because someone has uttered a fuzzy in need of clarification.

When Do We Use It?

So where does the goal analysis fit into the larger scheme of things? _Everywhere!_ When do we use the goal analysis procedure? Anytime these two conditions exist:

1. Someone describes an intent in abstract (fuzzy) terms, and
2. The intent is important to achieve.

Who Can Use the Goal Analysis Tool?

Just about everyone. Here are a few examples:

If you are a:	*You would use it whenever you accomplish or define what is meant by:*
CEO	"Maximize shareholder value" or "Create a strong competitive advantage."
Sales Manager	"Use a consultative selling approach" or "Have salespeople exude enthusiasm."
Technical Supervisor	"Be professional" or "Understand troubleshooting."
Quality Engineer	"Be quality conscious" or "Be a competent engineer."
Production Engineer	"Produce a quality product" or "Provide world-class service."
Instructor/Teacher	"Understand gas welding" or "Bc a good instructor."
Accounting Manager	"Appreciate investment principles" or "Be a detail person."

What Next?

Now that we know what a goal analysis is and when to use it, it's time to learn the procedure itself. Before we do, however, we need to know just what an abstraction (fuzzy) really represents. Without an understanding (oops—there goes one now) of the nature of an abstraction, it might be difficult to appreciate (there goes another one) just how important the goal analysis can be. So that's where we'll begin.

3
Where's Your Attitude?

What do physicians do when individuals ask, "Am I healthy?" How do they determine a state of health? What do they actually *do?* What they do is to check specifics. They take blood pressure, check eyes and ears, count pulse, check reflexes, and kick tires. And from information about *observable* things, they make statements about an abstract state—health. If the observable indicators look positive, physicians are willing to say that a person is healthy; that is, they are willing to generalize from the specific. But they don't ever check health directly. Health doesn't exist as a thing that can be probed, poked, or weighed. It is an abstract idea, the condition of which is *inferred* from visible specifics. Always.

Every statement about abstractions is inferred from visible or audible specifics. By definition, if an abstract term described something that was visible or audible, it wouldn't be abstract. That goes as much for statements about "attitude" as it does for statements about "motivation." It's as true for statements about "understanding" as it is for statements about "knowing."

Since it is worthwhile to be clear about this matter of abstractions versus specifics, let's think for a moment about "attitude." We might just as easily select any of the other common abstractions that we talk about (such as motivation, understanding, or self-concept), but we'll let attitude represent them all. What is true for attitude is true for every other abstraction.

So let's begin. Just what do we mean when we use the word *attitude?* Is attitude a *thing?*

Well, no. Not a thing like a meringue or a mukluk. *Things* are what you can poke with your fingers or beat with a stick. Attitudes are not that sort of thing. You can't dissect people and take out their attitudes any more than you can dissect them and take out their thoughts. That doesn't mean that attitudes and thinking don't exist; it's just that they aren't directly available for physical examination—or for poking or pinching.

So if attitude isn't a thing, what is it?

Attitude is a word, that's what it is. And words mean whatever their users want them to mean. (This one seems to have more misusers than users.)

By attitude, we generally mean to describe an abstraction, some sort of general state or condition existing inside ourselves or others. When I say, "She has a favorable attitude toward mukluks," I am suggesting that the person will behave in one way when faced with a mukluk rather than in another. I am suggesting that the mukluk-lover will tend to say favorable things about the object, that she will tend to move toward the object when she sees one rather than away from it, and that she will tend to seek out ways to come into contact with the object. Similarly, a person who is said to have a favorable attitude toward music would be expected to say favorable things about the sound, to respond favorably when in the presence of the sound, and to seek out ways of increasing the amount of time that he or she is in the presence of the sound.

It's a Prediction

An interesting thing about attitudes is that every statement about attitude is a statement of prediction. No matter what someone says about the attitude of someone else, he or she is making a prediction about how that person is likely to behave in the future. Based on what you have seen someone do or heard someone say in the past, you predict how he or she will perform in the future. If you see me turn a bowl of fish soup over the cook's head, you might be urged to comment: "He has a negative attitude toward fish soup." Such a comment is based on what you saw me do and is intended to predict that putting me in the presence of fish soup will be followed by some sort of negative act or comment on my part (toward the soup or the soupee). You might be right or wrong, but the statement about attitude is a statement of prediction, a statement that intends to suggest how I might behave in some future time.

Since an attitude is not directly visible, it follows that all statements about attitude are based on circumstantial evidence that takes the form of visible behavior. If you hadn't seen me dump the fish soup on the cook or heard or read an account of the fish story, you would have had no basis whatever for making a statement about how I am likely to behave in the presence of fish soup. You might be wrong in your attitude statement (your prediction); it might be the cook I dislike and not the fish soup. No problem; lots of people make incorrect predictions from the information available to them. The point is simply that, right or wrong, *a statement about attitude is a statement of prediction based on what somebody says or what somebody does.*

Indicator Behaviors

The behaviors on which attitude statements are based can properly be called *indicator behaviors,* for they are used as indicators of attitude. Indicators are common items of our existence. We use thermometers to indicate temperature, speedometers to indicate speed, and voltmeters to indicate voltage. In each case, we use some sort of device to tell us the state or condition of something we cannot see or measure directly.

Some indicators are better than others. A voltmeter is a better indicator of the amount of voltage present in an electrical circuit than the sensation you feel when you grab the wire. The loudness of your "ouch" is not directly related to the amount of the voltage.

The same holds true for attitudes and their indicator behaviors. Some behaviors are better indicators (predictors) of attitude than others, and it isn't always easy to tell which is better. To make it more difficult, any particular behavior might well be an indicator of any number of attitudes. When I poured the fish soup on the cook, he couldn't tell whether that behavior was indicating a distaste for fish soup, *his* version of fish soup, fur-lined soup bowls, dirty aprons, or him. In the absence of some other indicators (behaviors) on my part, he could predict pretty well *that* I found something distinctly not to my liking, but not *what*. He would need to observe more of my behavior if he wanted to be sure. If, while carrying out the deed, I spoke thusly: "Sir, my distaste for fish soup is exceeded only by my distaste for fish stew," he would have a better clue as to how to interpret my soup-pouring behavior.

So, for example, instead of merely noting that a person chews gum when she enters a classroom and then predicting, "She has a poor attitude about my course," it is more prudent to try to find at least several of the indicators that are representative of the attitude in which you are interested. If you know which performances you will accept as your meaning of an attitude or other goal, you will also know how to assess whether the attitude (tendency to perform one way rather than another) is in the condition you would like. You will also have clues about which performances to change in order to improve that condition; when someone changes what he or she does, others are likely to change the words they use to describe the person.

As an example, if a person has been labeled "hostile" because of his tendency to throw pies in the faces of his colleagues but later gives up this action, others are likely to stop calling him hostile and begin referring to him as reformed, or mellowed, or as having had a change of heart.

Notice that nothing in this discussion has had anything to do with behaviorism . . . or any other sort of ism. The concern with what people do and what they say does not stem from any sort of philosophical base. We are concerned with behavior (performance) because we have no other choice, no other route into the heart or mind of a person. It is the only sound basis we have for judgments about what is happening inside another human being. No matter how deeply we may desire that someone "develop a strong, positive self-concept" or "feel a deep and abiding appreciation for the value of eagles," the only evidence we have of the existence of such conditions is what the person says and does.

Since it is the *doing* that causes us to agree or disagree that some abstract state is present, it is the *doing* that matters most. So if you can figure out how to get people to do the things that represent the *definition* of a goal (abstract state), you will be in a much better position to achieve that goal. And that is the purpose of the goal analysis—to help you determine just what people would have to say or do for you to be willing to agree they had achieved the goal. Once you know what those "say and do" things are, you will find it much easier to figure out how to get them to happen.

Next?

Since knowing when to use a tool is a significant part of knowing how to use it, we'll begin with some practice in recognizing situations in which the goal analysis will help.

4
Recognizing Fuzzies

A manager had just reviewed a task analysis of an important position in his firm. "Yes," he said, "these are the skills we want performed in this job; but we also want the person to *communicate a positive attitude toward the company.*"

Now when we are talking about a skill, whether of the hand or of the mind, we can easily determine whether it exists in the shape we would like, and we can easily determine what to do to make it better. If we want to be better at batting, we would practice swinging a bat. If we want to be better at singing, we would sing. But suppose we want to be more successful or better human beings. Exactly what would we do to improve? Sing? Swing? Smile more? Get into another line of work? Hard to tell, isn't it?

Or suppose, as in the example described above, we want to be better at communicating a positive attitude. Would we study diction? Whistle while we work? Say nice things? We can't tell. It could be any or all of these things and perhaps dozens more.

The truth is that until we know what the person who wants to achieve this or any other goal *means* by the statement, we cannot decide how to achieve the state. Moreover, we cannot decide whether we are making progress or if we have been successful.

But that's not enough reason to use the goal analysis. After all, we spend a large part of our day speaking in fuzzies, and appropriately so.

"Good morning."
"Ah, good morning. Nice day, isn't it?"

That's a common interchange, intended to express friendship or courtesy. But hardly an appropriate time to reply with "Nice? Now *there's* a fuzzy. Just what do you mean by *that?*" Or:

"Ahhh, ma cherie, I loooove you."

Again, "What do you mean by *that?*" is hardly the correct reply. And so it goes. We often speak in generalities, and in most situations these abstractions are perfectly acceptable. But sometimes not. When the manager says, "We *must* improve our company image," or "You perform your tasks well, but you need to work on your attitude," *that's* when the goal analysis is used. When you say, "I must become more assertive," or "I want to be a better person," *that's* when the goal analysis is important. Whenever one of these abstractions (or *fuzzies*) shows up as something important enough to do something about, *then* is the time to use goal analysis. The goal analysis will unfuzzify the abstraction to the point where you can say whether there *is* any useful meaning, and if so, what the essence of that meaning might be.

Fuzzy-Watching Practice

Before reaching for the goal analysis tool, you need to know how to do two things:

1. Be able to recognize an abstraction when you see one, and

2. Decide whether that abstraction is important to achieve.

I can help you with the first; the second you will have to do for yourself. So here we go.

Intents to develop such states as "favorable attitudes," "deep appreciation," or "sense of pride" are examples of abstractions; they do not tell you what a person would be doing when demonstrating the state or condition, nor do they suggest the behavior that would indicate how you can tell that he or she has done it. On the other hand, items such as "writing," "decanting," and "hopping" are examples of performances; they *do* tell you what a person would be doing when demonstrating his or her ability to do it.

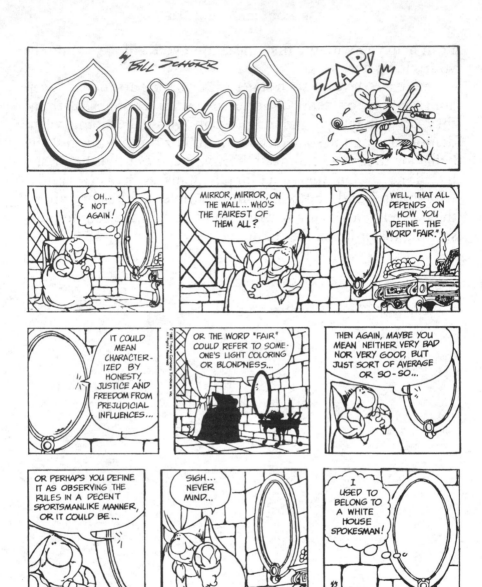

Reprinted by permission: Tribune Company Syndicate, Inc.

Let's check to see if we are thinking along the same lines.

Examine the intents listed below. Some are fuzzies (abstractions), and some are specifics (performances). *Check the fuzzies;* then read on to see how well we agree:

1. ___ interview an applicant

2. ___ appreciate music

3. ___ feel a sense of pride in one's work

4. ___ repair a trombone

5. ___ set a broken leg

6. ___ develop a sense of comradeship in attaining common goals

7. ___ edit a manuscript

8. ___ have a religious dedication to one's profession

9. ___ defend liberties

10. ___ write a report

11. ___ be a good citizen

Compare your responses with the comments on the pages that follow.

1. ____ interview an applicant

Can you tell whether someone is interviewing? Of course. Interviewing is directly observable, so you can call it a performance.

2. _✓_ appreciate music

What is someone doing when appreciating? Sighing? Breathing hard? Reciting the history of music? Playing a piece? The expression doesn't indicate or even imply the performances that constitute the meaning of the abstraction. This is a fuzzy.

3. _✓_ feel a sense of pride in one's work

Mmm . . . important, maybe. But in one's work, definitely not a performance. Ask the key question: "What would someone need to do to convince you that he or she had achieved this goal?" Those are the performances; this is a fuzzy.

4. ____ repair a trombone

Since you can see the repairing being performed, this is a performance.

5. ____ set a broken leg

Can you tell whether a person is setting a broken leg? Yes. You can see the steps of the task being performed. You may not be able to tell whether it is being done correctly, but you can tell that it is being done. A performance.

6. ✓ develop a sense of comradeship in attaining common goals

Ah, a beautiful sentiment and perhaps a worthwhile goal to attain, but definitely a goal and not a performance. Can you see people developing a sense of comradeship? Would everyone *agree* that what you see them doing is developing a sense of comradeship? Not likely. Another problem with this goal is that the word *develop* implies process; it implies that we're thinking about *how* the sense of comradeship will be attained, instead of what it will look like when it has been attained.

7. ____ edit a manuscript

This is a performance. You can tell if someone is editing. You may find that different editors behave differently when editing, but you can tell when they're editing. (My editor snickers ominously when slashing and thrusting at my words; others simply shake their heads while tsking.)

8. ✔ have a religious dedication to one's profession

This one is such an abstract abstraction I would even hesitate to give it the label of goal (it's more like a mission). It is of about the same caliber as "get the country moving again." The words have a lovely ring to them, but they don't provide the basis for making decisions about how we would know such a dedication if we saw one. "Having a dedication" isn't at all the same level of specificity as "having a baby."

9. ✔ defend liberties

Again, we have a nice-sounding goal. We can easily nod in agreement about its importance, but we would be hard put to say what to do to increase liberty-defending skills or recognize a liberty defender when we saw one. It doesn't matter that what a person might do to defend liberties is different in different situations; until we know what those things are, we can't make improvements.

10. _____ write a report

We may disagree about the criteria by which a given report should be judged, but there is not likely to be any disagreement about what someone is doing when writing a report. Writing is a performance that is directly visible (and often *audible*, if you find writing as hard as I do).

11. ✓ be a good citizen

This might be number one on the hit parade of fuzzies. It's certainly important, but what's a person doing when he or she is being a good citizen? What would you take as evidence that Sturmun Drang qualifies for the good-citizen award? Would it be different if he were a first grader than if he were a senior citizen?

Overt/Covert Performances

There are a few words that look like abstractions, but which are, in fact, performances. Words such as "identify," "discriminate," and "solve," for example, describe performances which are internal (covert); they describe actions that can be performed invisibly to the outside world. Just because they are invisible (covert) doesn't necessarily mean that they are abstractions.

Visible (overt) performances include behaviors such as hopping, singing, writing, and interviewing. These are things you can see people doing directly; you don't have to *infer* whether someone is doing these things because you can observe the performances directly. The existence of covert (invisible/cognitive) performances have to be inferred from things you see and hear people doing. How could you know someone has *recalled* a list of numbers? Or identified some fuzzies? You would have to ask them to do something visible or audible from which you can *infer* that the recalling or identifying has occurred.

So how can you tell the difference between covert performances and abstractions?

There is a simple test by which you can tell the difference between a performance and an abstraction. Find out whether there is a direct way to determine the nature of the alleged performance by asking this question:

> "Is there a *single* behavior or class of behaviors that will indicate the presence of the alleged performance, about which there would be general agreement?"

If the answer to the question is "yes," you have a performance. If it is "no," you are dealing with a fuzzy.

Let's try the test on a few likely candidates. If you believe an item to be a performance, see if you can jot down an answer to the key question. I've filled in the first one.

	What single act, if any, might you ask someone to perform that will tell you whether the condition exists?	*Is this item a performance?*
1. adding numbers	**Say (or write) the correct answer**	**Yes**
2. identifying piranhas		
3. appreciating values		
4. understanding computers		

Go on to the next page.

I would consider only the first two items to be performances. To find out if someone identified piranhas correctly, you could ask the person to point to the piranhas. That is a single act that would tell you directly if the internal performance occurred. You could also ask an individual to paint a red dot on each piranha or tap his or her finger on each of their heads. There are lots of *indicator behaviors* you could select from, so there is a direct way to sample the existence of the identifying.

But what *single* act would tell you whether anyone was appreciating values? Would everyone agree with the act you might select? Unlikely. And what single act would tell you whether there was an understanding of computers present? Making favorable comments about computers? Writing programs? Answering multiple-choice questions? Designing a computer? All of the above? None of the above? Would there be immediate agreement on the indicator you might select? Again, unlikely. Therefore, we would say of these items: "Value appreciation and computer understanding may be important goals to achieve, but they are not performances. If they *are* important to achieve, we must use the goal analysis to determine what to do to get the results we want."

One way to tell whether a statement is too broad to be considered a performance is to put the substance of the statement into the "Hey, Dad" Test. You simply use the substance of the statement to finish this sentence: "Hey, Dad, let me show you how I can _____!" If the result is absurd and makes you want to laugh, you are dealing with a statement broad enough to be considered an abstraction rather than a performance. For example: "Hey, Dad, let me show you how I can internalize my growing awareness!" (Yeah? Lemme see you!)

Silly, isn't it? That's because we aren't talking about a performance, either visible (external) or invisible (internal). We are talking about an abstraction. Try another example: "Hey, Dad, let me show you how I can be satisfied with my goals!" Not as funny, perhaps, but still rather odd. Now try this one:

"Hey, Dad, let me show you how I can smile!" Aha! Now that one has the ring of sense to it.

Try the "Hey, Dad" Test on the following items and see if it doesn't help you spot the performances from the abstractions:

- ride a bicycle

- add columns of numbers

- appreciate the value of gravity

- be warmed by success

- internalize the decision-making process

If you would like a little more practice in recognizing the difference between performances and abstractions, go to the next page.

Otherwise, go on to page 43.

Here are a few more items to help sharpen your ability to recognize performances and fuzzies. There are the usual three kinds of items on the list:

(1) visible or audible (overt) performances,

(2) invisible (covert) performances, and

(3) abstractions (fuzzies).

Check the fuzzies. Remember the key question: "Is there a single thing a person might do to convince me he or she is demonstrating the condition described in the item?"

1. ____ smiles a lot

2. ____ says favorable things about others

3. ____ feels deeply about others

4. ____ is confident in his or her ability

5. ____ can recognize symptoms

6. ____ is able to appreciate company policy

7. ____ is able to manage with enthusiasm

8. ____ knows how to compare prices

9. ____ can discriminate business trends

10. ____ is able to assemble components skillfully

Compare your responses to those on the pages that follow.

1. ____ smiles a lot

A performance. You can tell when someone is smiling. We don't know what "a lot" means, but that is another issue.

2. ____ says favorable things about others

Can you tell if someone is saying things about others? Yes. So this item can be called a performance.

3. ✓ feels deeply about others

What is someone doing when "feeling deeply?" We don't know and can't tell from the statement. A fuzzy. Perhaps important, but a fuzzy nonetheless.

4. ✓ is confident in his or her ability

Same as the last item.

5. ____ can recognize symptoms

Here is one of the covert performances. You may not be able to tell *whether* a person is recognizing at any point in time (he or she can stand around perfectly still while doing the recognizing), but you can tell whether the results of the recognizing are satisfactory or unsatisfactory. You can tell directly by asking the person to tell you something, point to something, label something, etc. The test is whether you can use a single indicator as evidence that the recognizing has occurred as desired.

6. ✓ is able to appreciate company policy

I'm sure *you* weren't fooled by the "is able to" opener, but there are still people who think that any sentence beginning with those words is automatically specific enough to be called a performance. That isn't the case at all, as this item illustrates. A fuzzy, not a performance.

7. ✓ is able to manage with enthusiasm

Same as for the previous item.

8. ✓ knows how to compare prices

This is a little bit of everything. "Knowing," of course, is an abstraction, but "comparing" is something else. Can you tell if someone compared? You could ask the person, who might reply, "Yes, I compared." But that isn't any better than if he or she said, "Yes, I know." Actually, there are a number of things someone might be doing when comparing—noting those things that are the same, finding the smallest or the largest, etc. Can you name an indicator behavior by which we will know if the comparing is acceptable? If you are not sure, or if there is room for disagreement, better think of this item more as a mini-fuzzy that will have to be defined further.

9. ✓ can discrimi-
nate business
trends

Similar to the last one. Again, because of the context, there is room for discussion about what "discriminate" means. Does this mean that someone divines trends, points to trends when they are shown on charts, or senses them during the flow of a business day? By itself, we would have to consider it an abstraction that needs further clarification before we could agree on what the person would be doing when doing it. If, however, there is a single indicator behavior that would satisfy you that a person could discriminate business trends, then you can consider "discriminate" to be a covert performance.

10. ___ is able to
assemble
components
skillfully

Can you tell what someone is doing when he or she is assembling? Yes. The person is putting things together. We don't know what "skillfully" means, but that doesn't matter, because "skillfully" is a word suggesting something about the criterion of acceptable performance, rather than a description of the performance itself.

Summary So Far

A goal is a statement describing a broad or abstract intent, state, or condition.

A goal analysis is useful whenever a goal exists that is important to achieve, or to achieve better than is presently the case. It is used whenever a statement of intent describes an abstraction, when the statement doesn't answer the question, "How will I know one when I see one?"

A performance is an activity that is directly visible or audible (overt), or directly assessable. An invisible or internal (covert) activity can also be considered a performance if it is directly assessable—that is, if there is a single behavior that will indicate the presence of the performance.

5
Getting It Down

It's time to plunge into the procedure itself, step by step. There are five steps, and each will be illustrated with examples from life. In brief, the steps are these:

1. Write down the goal.

2. List performances that exemplify goal achievement.

3. Sort the list and eliminate remaining fuzzies.

4. Describe performances in complete sentences.

5. Test for completeness.

After all the steps have been explained and illustrated, a chapter filled with examples—and a little practice—will follow. Finally, we'll consider some variations on a theme.

Before we begin, however, we should remind ourselves of these important points.

- Most goal analyses don't take very long to complete. When more than a few minutes are required, it's usually because time is needed to complete the list of performances that define the goal, because someone whose input is needed isn't immediately available, or because consensus on the goal meaning has to be reached.

- It is easy to confuse process and results (outcomes). The activities associated with goal achievement are these:

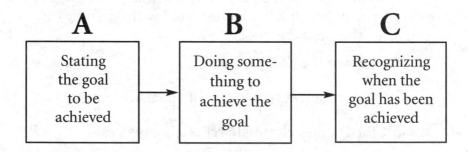

A

Stating the goal to be achieved

B

Doing something to achieve the goal

C

Recognizing when the goal has been achieved

Our concern in this book is with Items A and C, because until we know how to recognize our destination (achievement of the goal), we don't know what to do to get there. The procedure for achieving goals, then, is first to say what the goal is (A), then to describe how goal accomplishment will be recognized (C), and finally to take action (B). Here's how:

Step One

Write Down the Goal.

Use whatever words are comfortable, regardless of how fuzzy or vague they may be. This is the place for such words. The reason it doesn't matter how broad the words are here is that this step is just to get you started and to help you remember what caused you to start analyzing in the first place. For example, you might write items like these:

- The incumbents should have a good attitude regarding their constituents.
- have pride in work
- have an awareness of civic responsibility
- appreciate the legal system
- have a successful marriage
- experience successful industrial relations

Note that the first item looks like a complete sentence, and the others are more like scraps of sentences. No matter. Use the words that make you (or the person for whom you are doing the goal analysis) feel good. If you can make yourself feel good as soon as you begin, you may be more likely to continue.

There is another reason why it is useful to begin a goal analysis by writing down the goal. It is "politically" useful. People can almost always agree with each other on the importance of vaguely stated intentions. They will all tend to agree that things like "good customer relations," "good citizenship," and "ethical conduct" are fine things to have. They will not necessarily always agree on the specific actions that should represent the definition of those things. And if they see only your list of specifics, they may very well accuse you of doing "trivial" things. So write the goal on top of the page. A good place to begin, good window dressing . . . but don't get too attached to the wording, because the process of analysis may show you the sense of taking another direction.

Caution

There is only one caution about how to state the goal. Make sure your statement describes an intended *outcome* rather than a *process.* That way, you won't get bogged down with the problem of means and ends before you get started. Once you know what you are trying to attain, *then* you can think about the best means of getting there. So, make your goals talk about the ends rather than the means of attaining those ends. Make the statement say "*have* a favorable attitude toward barnacles" rather than "*learn* to have a favorable attitude toward barnacles." Make it read "*understand* foreign trade" rather than "*develop* an understanding of foreign trade."

To give you a little practice in making goals describe ends rather than means, here are a few practice items. Each item is now stated in a way that will get the analyst in trouble, because it implies something about how the goal is achieved rather than about *what* the goal state to be achieved is. Fix each item by making it describe ends—that is, cross out the words implying process and replace them with words implying outcomes.

1. Develop a fuller appreciation of the concept of détente.

2. Grow to discover a yearning for classical music.

3. Come to see that the pollution problem is important.

4. Develop a sense of humor.

5. Reach the maturity needed to have a favorable attitude toward customers.

Turn to the next page to see if we agree.

When fixed, this is what the items on the previous page should look like:

1. Appreciate the concept of détente.

2. Have a yearning for classical music.

   or

   Have a favorable attitude toward classical music.

3. Understand the importance of the pollution problem.

   or

   Appreciate the problem of pollution.

4. Have a sense of humor.

5. Have a favorable attitude toward customers.

NOTE: It is always useful to name the "who," the people whose performance is the reason for the goal analysis. For example, the actions representing safety consciousness are one thing for truck drivers and something quite different for accountants. For another example, when managers say, "I want my people to be more responsible," a goal analysis would be far more successful when "my people" is identified. Responsible actions in a laboratory might be quite different from those required by computer programmers.

Before proceeding with a goal analysis, therefore, be clear about whose performance is at issue.

So, the first step in goal analysis is to write down the goal, making sure it describes an intended outcome rather than the means for reaching that outcome.

Step Two

Write Down Everything Someone Would Have to Say or Do for You to Agree He or She Represents Achievement of the Goal.

Without editing or judging, jot down everything that can possibly represent the meaning of the goal. Use only words or phrases and make no attempt to tidy things up as you go. (Tidying will come later.) Just remember this rule: *First you get it down, and then you get it good.*

The reason you must complete this step without being judgmental is that it is the most difficult step to complete, not so much because it's hard to understand, but because it takes time to think through the cloud of fuzzies to the specifics you are searching for. Usually, when we ask ourselves for the meaning of an abstraction, we answer ourselves in yet another abstraction. It just takes a little time to get used to the process of listing performances—instead of abstractions.

So write down everything that comes to mind. We'll sort it all out in Step Three.

Five Strategies

Here are five strategies for getting things down that may help you complete Step Two (describing the meaning of your goal). Use whichever is most productive for you.

1. Answer the question, "What will I take as evidence that my goal has been achieved?" What would cause you to be willing to stamp a person with the label of your goal? If you want a favorable attitude toward school, for example, what would it take to make you agree that the attitude of Jeremy Jimperly is in the shape you would like it

to be? Jot down everything that you can think of, without any concern for the fact that many of the items are just as broad as the one you started with, without any concern for the suspicion that some items may not make the best of sense. If it will help, write the rule on the very top of your page: *First you get it* down, *then you get it* good.

After all, you can't repair what you don't have. You can't cross out things that aren't there. You can't rearrange invisible items. Besides, thinking about what you would accept as evidence of achievement of your goal is hard enough without complicating the matter by having to write down only the things that make sense.

2. Answer the question, "Given a room full of people, what is the basis on which I would separate them into two piles—those who had achieved my goal and those who had not?" After all, you *do* make judgments about whether your students or trainees are acceptable in skill or attitude; you do make statements about their understanding or motivation or feeling. Now is the time to lay on the table the basis for those statements.

3. There is still another way to think about the performances that demonstrate the meaning of your goal. Imagine that someone else will be charged with the responsibility for deciding which of your students will be labeled with the goal and which will not be so labeled, and that you are going to tell this person how to proceed. What will your instructions be? What should he or she look for? *How will the person know a goal achiever when he or she sees one?* Suppose you want people who are conscientious. Never mind for the moment how they get that way or what you might do to achieve that state.

Given a room full of people, how would you separate them into two piles—those who had and those who had not achieved the goal?

Think about the state itself and how you would tell someone how to recognize it. Should your looker look for people who:

- finish their work on time?
- ask for extra assignments?
- work neatly?
- stay until their work is completed?

Jot down all the clues you can think of. (Or, if you are the literate type, all the clues of which you can think.)

4. Think of someone who is one and write down why you think so. That is, think of a person who already has achieved your goal, someone who represents your goal, and write down the things he or she says and does that cause you to be willing to pin the goal label on this person. If, for example, your goal is to have trainees "demonstrate pride in their work," think of someone who demonstrates pride in his or her work and write down the performances that cause you to say this person has your kind of pride. If you can*not* think of anyone who represents your goal, you have a problem. Perhaps your expectations are unreasonable. Perhaps the goal (as you perceive it) is unattainable. If so, then a change in expectation is in order.

If you cannot think of a real person who represents your goal, ask yourself this question: "Is it reasonable or practical to expect to achieve this goal?" If the answer is "no," revise the goal to one that is reasonable and practical to achieve. If the answer is "yes," and you still cannot think of someone who represents the state or condition described by the goal, you need to think of what a person *might* be like if he or she represented your goal. You are skating on thin ice, though, because when you think of hypothetical people, there is the danger that your expectations will be forever unattainable. It's much better to think of real people and to state why you are willing to point your finger in their direction and say they exemplify your goal. Suppose, for example, you want students "to be able to write effectively." Having written the goal, you would think of someone you know who writes effectively enough to suit you; then you would ask yourself *why* you are willing to say so. What does this person say or do that makes you willing to say he or she writes effectively? Could it be that the person:

- uses good grammar?
- uses descriptive words?
- expresses ideas in the fewest possible words?
- gets desired results?
- gets a reader to repeat his or her ideas with relative accuracy?

BONER'S ARK   **By ADDISON**

Whatever you think might be the basis for your judgment, write it down.

5. Try the back door. If all else fails, here's a sure-fire way to get started. Just write down all the reasons you would *never* point to someone and say, "This person represents the goal." What behaviors, or absence of behaviors, would cause you to say, "This is *not* someone who has achieved this goal, and this is why."

    For example, suppose the goal is "Be a sensitive and caring spouse," and you're having trouble describing what such a person would be like in performance terms. OK. Go in through the back door, and tell yourself what an *in*sensitive clod would be likely to do or not do. Would any of the following behaviors fit?

    -   kicks sand in spouse's face.
    -   never says, "I love you."
    -   pokes fun at spouse's opinions.
    -   reads the comics during sex.

    Once you've listed the negatives, it's no trick to turn them into positive statements describing the things a sensitive person does, and doesn't, do. There is an added benefit to the back-door aproach; not only is it a sure-fire way to get started, it will also lead to some giggles—especially if you're doing the analysis with someone else.

Examples from the Positive

Safety Consciousness. This example comes from a group of industry managers whose company had an accident record higher than they thought reasonable. The showing of safety films and the display of safety posters didn't seem to have much effect. The managers decided they wanted to be more successful in achieving safety consciousness in their employees, so they decided to take a closer look at this goal. Following the procedure described in Step One, they wrote the goal on a flip chart: "Be Safety Conscious."

The next step was to remind each other of the things they would take as evidence of safety consciousness, to tell each other the things that safety-conscious people say and do.

"Well," said one manager, "I think of old Joe Carson as being safety conscious, because he reports safety hazards whenever he sees them."

"Yes," said another, "and he wears his safety equipment."

A third then added, "A safety-conscious person is one who follows safety rules, whether they are posted or not. That is, he or she adheres to what is generally considered safe practice."

And so it went. Each item mentioned was written on the flip chart as a potential part of what these managers *meant* by safety consciousness. After half an hour or so, their list looked something like this:

<u>Be Safety Conscious</u>
- reports safety hazards
- wears safety equipment
- follows safety rules (no infractions)
- practices good housekeeping (keeps work area free of dirt, grease, and tools)
- encourages safe practice in others (reminds others to wear safety equipment)
- says favorable things about safe practice
- suggests ways to improve safety record

This, then, was the main basis for deciding whether a person was safety conscious or not. These were the performances that would cause a manager to pin the label of "safety consciousness" on someone. This was therefore the essence of the managers' *meaning* of the goal of safety consciousness.

Pride in Work. Here is an example of a more difficult goal, one that proved harder to define. The faculty of a dental school decided that a very important goal for their graduates to achieve was "pride in work." They explained, somewhat facetiously, that they didn't want their graduates leaning over their patients muttering things like ". . . y'know . . . I never *really* wanted to be a dentist in the first place." Though not meant to be taken seriously, the comment did suggest something about what this faculty meant by *lack* of pride.

After writing down the goal "Have pride in work," the faculty members began to think of the things student dentists might say or do to make their teachers willing to pin this label on them. In this case, as in many others, it wasn't easy to get started. After all, though people often talk to each other in the broad terms of goal language, they seldom think very seriously about just exactly what they mean by those nice words.

After considering that (a) the group was just trying to put down *possibilities* from which to select and (b) there was no need for agreement about what was put down, one of the members offered an opening shot: "Well, at least *I* would never say student dentists had pride in their work if they didn't do their assigned work on time." (If this sounds a little defensive, it is probably because people aren't used to being challenged to expose the basis for their judgment, especially on such affective matters as "pride in work." So, if you are ever in a position to help people define their goals, write down *whatever* is said quickly, and in the old brainstorming manner, refrain from passing judgment on what is said. [That comes later.])

Once the ice was broken, a half-hour of discussion produced the following jottings:

Have Pride in Work (dental students)
- carries out assigned tasks on time
- finishes tasks regardless of the time required
- carries out tasks regardless of whether others carry out theirs
- finishes, or reports, unfinished tasks left by others
- carries out tasks completely, leaving no loose ends
- performs most tasks at maximum personal ability level
- speaks favorably about the profession
- speaks favorably about well-performed tasks
- dresses in a manner befitting the profession

You can see that for this group the essence of "pride in work" had mainly to do with how tasks are carried out. _You_ may mean something completely different, and others may have still other meanings (if that were _not_ the case, there would be no need to clarify goals). But this faculty has done everyone the courtesy of making _their_ meaning visible. _Now_ they are in a position to discuss their meaning, to decide whether it is the best meaning for their situation, and to write the objectives that embody the essence of the meaning. And once they've done that, they can act to achieve their goal more effectively than ever before.

Love of Learning. Instructors are frequently heard to say that they want their students to have a "favorable attitude toward learning." This is an admirable intention, provided that instructors then take care to do the things that will enhance such an attitude rather than detract from it. The first step toward such an accomplishment is to make sure that instructors know in detail what students should do or say if they are to be representative of a favorable attitude toward learning.

One group of instructors went about it this way. They first listed the _names_ of students they knew who, they all agreed, had a favorable attitude toward learning. Then they began to tell each other what it was these students did or said that qualified them for the "favorable attitude" label. They reminded each other that "anything goes" during this phase of the analysis, and their first list looked like this:

Favorable Attitude Toward Learning
- shows up when expected
- is prepared to work (brings his or her stuff)
- asks questions when in doubt
- does more than the minimum required
- makes suggestions for improvement of the instruction
- helps teach others
- has initiative
- is a self-starter
- is eager and dedicated

Notice that the list trailed off into some fuzzies. This almost always happens, which is why Step Three (the sorting-out step) follows Step Two.

Notice also that even though the goal analysis was not complete at this point, these instructors already had developed some good clues about how to increase favorable attitude. For example, if one of the things they want students to do is to ask questions when in doubt, then the instructors need to make certain that question-asking behavior isn't punished, either intentionally or accidentally. In other words, instructors can increase the number of questions asked by responding to questions in a way that the students consider favorable.

For now, however, the task was to find out just what behaviors (performances) the instructors wanted to see more of and what they wanted to see less of.

Examples from the Negative

As I said earlier, sometimes it isn't easy to get started scratch-papering down the performances that represent the achievement of your goal; sometimes it isn't easy to start describing how to recognize a goal achiever when you see one. Oh, well. If you can't get in the front door, try the back. If you can't get started by describing the positive, try the negative. You can *always* think of several performances that are clearly *excluded* from your meaning of a goal. You can always think of things a person might do or say that would cause you to say, "*That* is certainly *not* representative of a person who _____." For example:

"I would never think of myself as successful if I hadn't stopped smoking."

"I would never agree that people understand the fundamentals of economics if they keep their life savings in a bank."

"Employees with a favorable attitude toward customers don't ignore customers who ask for help."

Once you have started listing the performances that you don't want to see, you can usually turn them into the positive without much difficulty.

Good Personality. Let me illustrate how this works with an example developed with some hotel managers who wanted their bartenders to have a "good personality." If any goal ever qualified as a fuzzy, this is it. Suppose someone handed you a clump of students and said, "Here. Go teach these people to have a good personality." What would you teach them? Where would you begin? How would you know if your instruction had succeeded?

You may not care much about the personality of bartenders, but those who employ them and those who use their services do. (Bars used to be just places to gather for a bit of friendly banter and good cheer; now they seem to be more like group-therapy centers.)

The attempt to think of the performances that would cause the managers to agree a bartender had a good personality left them nothing but blank paper. They couldn't for the life of them get started listing the things that would cause them to point at someone and proclaim "good personality."

So, we tried from the other end:

"Have you ever fired a bartender?" they were asked.

"Have we ever!" was the reply.

"Tell us about them" was the request.

And they did. Within minutes, the hotel managers listed a half-dozen characteristics of the *un*acceptable bartender:

The Acceptable Bartender is Not:
- sour
- humorless
- abrupt
- blameful of customer
- aggressive
- of gloomy appearance

Could you help but notice that all the items on this list are fuzzies? You will often find this to be the case. But first drafts are for getting down, not for getting good. Don't worry about what the first try looks like, because there is a way to handle the problem. Simply put each fuzzy on a separate sheet of paper and start over; repeat the process until you reach the performances that are the essence of your meaning. The hotel managers did that with their negative fuzzies, and they turned them positive as they went. Before long, they had statements like these:

1. Handles glasses with care, without spilling or slamming.

2. Smiles visibly when serving or addressing customers.

And as soon as they had these statements written down, they said, "But wait a minute. Those things don't have anything to do with good personality!" And maybe they were right.

But who cares? Vague terms are interchangeable, and "good personality" was just a place to start. There are any number of other goals they might have started with that would have served as well, such as "friendly person," "empathetic with customers," or even "be a good Joe." The key issue was whether the two statements they came up with represented important performances.

The managers then said, "But wait a minute. Those performances are trivial!" The reply to this charge is that the test of triviality is not in the words *describing* a performance. You cannot tell whether the item is trivial merely by reading it. *The test of triviality is in the consequence of not achieving the performance.* If there is no consequence when the performance is absent, one might well entertain the thought of triviality.

But if there is a consequence, then the performance is not trivial, no matter what words are used to describe it. In the case of the present example, the conversation went something like this:

"What happens to bartenders who spill stuff on hotel customers?"

"We *fire* them."

"What happens if bartenders don't smile regularly?"

"We fire them, too."

What is trivial about being fired? That is really something in the way of a consequence. Since it *matters* whether they are careful and smiley, these performances are not trivial, regardless of how the bartender might feel inside; therefore, the statements that will ultimately describe these intended outcomes will not be trivial either. It doesn't matter whether the words are long ones or short ones; the test of triviality is not in the words but in the consequence.

The Good Teacher. How many times have you heard someone say, "You can't define a good teacher"? Or, "Nobody can say what a good teacher is"? Actually, those are pretty silly statements; they imply that if you can't do something perfectly, you can't do it at all. But try it this way: Can you think of anything that a "good teacher" (whatever that means) *doesn't do?* Of course you can. Lots of things. And if you can list things that are *un*acceptable, you have a good beginning of a description of what is acceptable or desirable. How about these as examples of what good teachers *don't* do:

- keep students in the dark about what is expected of them
- use language or examples that are inappropriate for their audience
- punish students for doing the very things they are expected to do

How about adding a few yourself? Think about the things that turned you off or got in the way of your learning when you were in school. Then add them to my list. Once you've done that and turned the statements positive, you've gone a long way toward describing what many feel is indescribable.

Summary So Far

The first two steps in the goal analysis procedure are these:

Step One: *Write down the goal, using whatever words best describe the intended outcome.*

Step Two: *Write down the performances that would cause you to agree the goal had been achieved, without regard for duplication or fuzzinaciousness.*

6
Sorting It Out

Once you've jotted down the things you think might cause you to agree your goal had been achieved, you will need to go back over your list and do some tidying up and sorting out. Why? Because if your list is anything like the ones I've seen or developed, there will be all sorts of cats and dogs on it. For one thing, you are almost certain to find items that are at least as broad or abstract as the one you started with. Those who begin to say what they mean by "initiative," for example, often write down "is responsible." Similarly, those who begin to say what they mean by "is responsible" write down "takes the initiative."

This is not difficult to understand. In conversation we use lots of words that either say the same thing or nothing at all. Lots of vague terms are interchangeable, you see, so there are bound to be a number of fuzzies making their way onto your list. "We want our students to be conscientious," we say. Oh, and what does that mean? Why, it means we want them to be responsible. And what does "responsible" mean? Well, it means we want them to have pride in their work. And *that* means we want them to be dedicated. And around and around we go, defining one fuzzy with another. Little wonder we don't experience as much success with the so-called affective domain as we'd like.

On your list you may also find redundancies or duplications, things you have said in more than one way. In addition, you may find some items that, on second thought, can be crossed out simply because they don't say what you want to say.

You may occasionally find some items that describe procedure rather than outcomes, means rather than ends. These are to be deleted, for the object of the analysis is to figure out how to know an outcome when you see one, not how to make one happen.

Step Three

Sort the Items Listed in Step Two.

1. Cross out duplications and items that, on second thought, do not represent the meaning of your goal.

2. Place check marks beside the items that do not qualify as performances; that is, check the fuzzies.

3. Make sure all remaining or unmarked items describe outcomes rather than processes.

The checked items (the fuzzies) will each be put onto a separate piece of paper and treated just like a new goal. Performances will be listed and sorted until your entire list consists only of performances—things you can tell if someone is doing or not doing.

Example: Initiative

Here's an example of how it goes. While working toward analysis of a goal described as "demonstrates initiative," a group of managers listed the following items during Step Two (in this case they were referring to first-level supervisors):

- enjoys responsibility
- makes good decisions
- uses good judgment
- is on time

After completing the list, they went through the items for sorting. The first item is a double fuzzy. Both words ("enjoys" and "responsibility") describe general states. Both are inferred from the things you might see someone do or say. Since the managers agreed that this was an important item for further consideration, they labeled it a goal and went to the next item.

They thought about the second and third items. Both were fuzzies, but although good judgment was an important quality, they felt that what they were really interested in was good decision-making. Since good decision-making was the main thing they meant by good judgment, they threw out the latter item as being essentially a duplication of the former.

Finally, they thought about the last item. "Yes," they said, "we can tell directly if a person is on time. One is either there at the appointed hour or one isn't. All we have to do is say what we mean by 'on time,' so that a criterion of acceptable performance will be available." That was easier said than done, however, for there was quite a discussion about just what the limits of "on-timeness" should be. But that was real progress, since they were now discussing the desired shape of a performance rather than arguing about abstractions.

Reworking their list, they now had:

✓ *enjoys responsibility*

✓ *makes good decisions*

  is on time

The first two items, having been checked as goals, were put on separate pieces of paper; a new analysis was begun for each.

The third item, already qualifying as a performance, was shelved until the performances defining the first two goals were identified. Once that was done, the managers were ready for the final steps in the goal analysis procedure.

The list for "enjoys responsibility" looked like this:

- accepts new assignments without complaint
- appears on time for management meetings
- keeps subordinates informed
- meets deadlines
- spends time managing instead of operating

An explanation of the last item is in order. The rule of thumb in industry seems to be: Promote the best operators to supervisory level, but don't teach them how to supervise. As a result, there are thousands of supervisors who are good at their old jobs, whatever the jobs were, but who are totally insecure about managing. The end result is that they tend to spend time doing what they did before they were promoted, because it's what they know how to do.

The list for "makes good decisions" looked like this:

- identifies company goals supported by decisions
- always informs subordinates of decisions, and the reasons for making them
- makes decisions in time to be useful
- keeps well-informed about company goals and plans

Notice that the last item looks more like process than outcome—that is, it looks like one of the things one might do to become a good decision-maker. Once that fact was pointed out, the item was stricken from the list. The two lists were then combined, and further discussion was focused on clarifying the performances.

Example: Honest Reporting

Here is an interesting example of a goal analysis, interesting because it began with a very profound-sounding goal and ended with a list of very measurable performances.

In a large company that employs a substantial number of maintenance people (sometimes called customer engineers, technical representatives, or maintenance crew), management noticed that the information flowing from the field to the company was often erroneous or non-existent. The reports filed after machine repair were used as the basis for several important decisions; but, it was said, those reports were completed in a shabby fashion.

"We need more honest reporting," said management. Suppose you were faced with the assignment of increasing the honesty of the reporting. What would you do? Give lectures on ethics? Extol the importance of company policy? Make examples of those whose reports were not honest? Needless to say, you wouldn't know *what* action to take until you knew the results you wanted to achieve.

In this case two managers sat down to decide just what it was that was wanted. And this is an important point. They didn't sit down to figure out what THE meaning of honesty was, that is, to describe the ultimate definition of honest reporting. They sat down to describe their own desired outcomes. The demand for more honest reporting was what got them started, but they didn't feel enslaved to the words that just happened to be used by those voicing the complaint.

"How would we know if we had honest reporting?" was the question that began the analysis. But before long, the list looked like this:

- accurate
- valid
- complete
- reviewed for corrections

- properly distributed
- promptly filed
- exhibits good report-writing attitude
- legibly written

Notice that what had started out as an analysis of "honest reporting" quickly turned into an analysis of "Proper Maintenance Report." (Thinking does wonders.)

When sorting this list, they quickly deleted "exhibits good report-writing attitude"; they realized that "reviewed for corrections" and "properly distributed" were important but didn't describe characteristics of the report itself. Further discussion clarified the meaning of the performances, after which they drafted their final product. It said nothing whatever about honesty, as that turned out not to be the issue. The issue was the shape of the report. Here's what they ended up with:

The Characteristics of a Proper Maintenance Report

1. All information is recorded in the correct place.

2. All information is true.

3. All information is relevant to the problem
    (no superfluous information is recorded).

4. All information is legible.

5. All boxes are checked or filled.

6. All maintenance actions are recorded.

7. Report is reviewed and signed by the customer.

8. One copy each of the report is:
    a. sent to the district office
    b. given to the customer, and
    c. attached to the failed component, if any.

What began as an alleged problem with morals or ethics was seen, through goal analysis, to be a simple problem of communication. Once the problem description was turned into a checklist and distributed to the maintenance staff, the quality of the reports improved.

Did you notice that one of the items on the list was a negative—that is, it called for the *absence* of superfluous information? Again, I want to repeat that you will often encounter instances in which you expect to determine whether someone has achieved a particular goal by noting the *absence* of behavior. No need to be concerned, now that you are forewarned. After all, there is nothing wrong with defining a goal in terms of the *absence* of behaviors (note how many of the Ten Commandments call for non-behavior) if that is what you intend to mean.

Also, did you notice that this list describes the results of performance, rather than the performance itself? And that the list talks about the characteristics of the completed report, rather than the behaviors (actions) used in preparing the report? Again, no problem. Once again, the purpose of the goal analysis is to help you to describe what things would be like if, in fact, the goal were achieved. If the way to get to that is to describe the products of the behaviors rather than the behaviors themselves, fine.

Sometimes, after completing a goal analysis, people will say, "Wait a minute. We've said what things would be like when the goal is achieved, but is that *right*? Should we adopt a *different* meaning of the goal?" Notice that this question can only arise after you've made the components of goal achievement visible (written down). If that makes you want to "improve" your goal definition, fine. But that is an issue beyond the scope of this book.

Summary So Far

The goal analysis procedure so far, then, is this:

Step One: *Write down the goal in outcome terms.*

Step Two: *Jot down the performances that, if observed, would cause you to agree the goal has been achieved.*

Step Three: *Once a goal has been written and a list has been drafted of the things you think would cause you to agree the goal had been achieved, sort out the list. Delete duplications and the items that, on second thoughts, are unwanted. Check abstractions, and mark performances in some other handy-dandy fashion. Then write each remaining goal (abstraction) on a separate piece of paper. Repeat the process until every item remaining is either a performance or a non-performance: either a "does it" or a "doesn't do it."*

7
Putting It Together

We do goal analyses to help us decide what actions to take to be more successful at achieving those goals. We do it because we want to know what steps to take to get closer to goal achievement, rather than because we enjoy sitting around defining terms. For this reason there are still two steps to complete. These steps will help put boundaries, or limits, around the performances and tell you when you are done with the analysis.

Step Four

Write a Complete Sentence to Describe Each of the Items on Your Final List.

Each sentence will describe an outcome that must be achieved for you to be willing to say your goal is reached. This step will make it easier to test these outcomes to see if they truly reflect what you mean by the goal, and it will help you decide what to do next.

For example, after completing the first three steps of a goal analysis on "good reporting," the manager of a research division came up with this list of performances:

- identifies routing
- determines presentation form
- writes report
- presents report

Though that is a good start, it isn't precise enough to tell us what to do next. Though each item is a performance, it doesn't tell us how to know whether the performance is present or absent. When this manager completed Step Four, his analysis looked like this:

Good Reporting

1. For each report, be able to name the members of senior management to whom copies of the report should be directed.

2. For each report, be able to determine (name) the form of presentation that will most clearly communicate the content to a non-scientific audience.

3. Be able to prepare a written report that summarizes all of the findings, conclusions, and recommendations bearing on the researched issue.

4. Be able to report (orally) to the appropriate members of senior management, providing them with all the information they need to take effective action.

Note that these statements tell us *what* is expected to be done, and they tell us something about *how well* people are expected to do it. With these complete sentences in hand, it was possible for the manager to determine which scientists had the skill to perform each of these items and to decide what action to take in those instances where the skill was lacking. In other words, what might have started as a grumbling exercise about the lack of "good reporting" ended up—through goal analysis—with a blueprint for action.

Take Me to Your Leader

Here's another example, this one from a comprehensive analysis of one of those superfuzzies—"good leadership." One of the items on the original list said something like "Knows how not to reward counter-productive or disruptive behavior." That isn't too bad all by itself, but in this case the analysts went much further. Their Step Four list for this one performance, a mini-fuzzy really, looked like this:

1. Can identify (point to) counter-productive or disruptive behaviors.

2. Can specify and implement techniques for monitoring the occurrence of counter-productive or disruptive behaviors.

3. Can design and implement techniques for eliminating the inadvertent reinforcers of such behaviors.

4. Can modify a reinforcement (reward) program if desired changes fail to occur.

With these descriptions of intended outcomes in hand, they were able (a) to determine whether each of the outcomes was happening to their satisfaction, and if not, (b) to decide what to do about it.

As you read these examples, keep in mind that the analysts were not looking for some sort of supermeaning—some sort

of "one and only" meaning—for their goals. There were looking for what the goal means to them in their situation. Any
search for the one and only meaning is rather like hunting for
a handle on a fog: There is no such thing. It is for this very reason also that it doesn't pay to get too involved with the goal
words you start with. Since there are so many other words you
could have used, and since it is a *practical* rather than an *ultimate* meaning that is being sought, your starting words may
quickly fall by the wayside. If they do, let them fall. And rejoice,
because it means you are getting closer to something you can
do something about.

The task during Step Four, then, is to write as clear a
description as you can of each desired performance. Usually
this will take the form of a single sentence; sometimes it will
require two or more sentences.

Step Five

Test the Sentences for Completeness.

In other words, test your collection of sentences to see
whether you have finished the analysis. This is done by looking at the collection of sentences and asking, "If all these things
occurred as described, would I be willing to say that the goal
had been achieved?" If the answer is "yes," then the analysis is
finished and you are ready to decide what you need to do to
make sure those performances occur as desired. If the answer
is "no," then you need to answer this question: "What else
would have to happen before I would agree the goal had been
achieved?" Add that "something else" to your list, then ask the
first question again: "Now would I be willing to agree the goal
was achieved if the things on this list happened?" If not, you
need to keep searching for the missing item(s). When, at last,
you utter a jubilant (or reluctant) "Yes!" to the key question,
you will be finished.

Here are some examples to show how Step Five works:

A Case of Consciousness

The goal was for production employees to be "more security conscious," because the plant manufactured classified military products. During the second step of the analysis, the managers doing the work quickly discovered that their main concern was with the way in which sensitive documents, such as blueprints, were handled. When they had finished the third step, they had written:

Security Conscious

- does not leave classified documents unattended
- locks up materials

Though these statements describe things you might see a person doing or not doing, they do not answer the question "What will you take as evidence the goal has been achieved?" They do not yet say how to tell when someone does or does not perform as desired. The managers who completed this analysis quickly understood the problem; they asked each other what would be a reasonable expectation with regard to the desired performances. Before long, the following statements were drafted (thus completing Step Four of the analysis):

A person is said to be security conscious when:

1. There are no instances in which he or she has been found to leave sensitive documents unattended.

2. His or her filing cabinet is always found locked when unattended (when the employee leaves for the day or leaves the room in which the cabinet is located).

How will the managers know a security-conscious employee when they see one? They will know one when they find a person who has never left sensitive documents unattended and whose files are always locked during his or her absences. That person will be called "security conscious." Anyone for whom they have counted one or more instances of unattended documents or open files will not be considered "security conscious."

They were then ready for Step Five, the last step in the goal analysis procedure; testing the statements for adequacy. The managers asked themselves if they would be willing to say an employee was "security conscious" if the person locked his or her files and didn't leave classified documents unattended. Their answer was "Well, yes; but only insofar as the care of documents is concerned." Therefore, they were finished with that part of their analysis. If, on the other hand, their answer had been "no," they would have had to find out what was missing in their meaning of the goal. They would have had to find the missing essence of their meaning of the goal.

Now that the managers had a clear idea of what they were looking for, they were in a position to do two things they couldn't do before: (1) determine the current extent of security consciousness (i.e., count the number of employees who were security conscious according to their own definition); and (2) decide what actions to take to increase that number. And *that* is precisely what the analysis is for.

A Case of Gas

This example was developed by a high-school instructor who wanted his students to "understand gas welding." As you might guess, this teacher worked in a vocation area, and he wanted his students to be able to have a comprehensive knowledge (there's a nice fuzzy for you) of the subject. His initial list of items had several fuzzies on it, such as "know how gas is

produced," "understand metals," and "appreciate flame adjustment." Sorting led him to identify and delete the performances
that he was not concerned about. When he drafted statements
about each performance he was concerned about, his meaning
of "understanding" turned out to be:

The student who understands gas welding is able to:

1. Explain production of oxygen and acetylene gases.

2. Explain methods and precautions to be observed while
    handling oxygen and acetylene cylinders and equipment.

3. Assemble gas-welding components to the cylinders.
    Components will include regulators, hoses, blowpipes,
    and tips.

4. Select proper tip and oxygen-acetylene pressures for
    work pieces of the following type (list added).

5. Adjust work piece and blowpipe-tip handle for the flat
    welding position.

6. Light the torch and adjust to a neutral flame.

7. Establish and complete the weld while observing proper
    pattern and ending of the weld.

8. Shut down the welding unit and prepare it for storage.

Carrying out the final step, the test for adequacy, he asked
himself the question: "If students did all these things, would I
be willing to say that they understood gas welding?" His
answer was "yes," so his analysis was finished. Now he was in a
position (1) to determine the number of students who currently understood to his satisfaction and (2) to take steps to
increase that number.

There are any number of things that one might mean by "understands gas welding," as you might guess. One might mean knowing the history of welding, knowing who is who in the welding business, and so on. Some people think that because the subject being taught is vocational, technical, or professional, it is therefore patently obvious what must be taught. This simply isn't true. In any subject area, there are a great many possible answers to the question, "What is worth teaching?"

A Case of Creativity

Some of those who have, in my opinion, done the best job of defining their affective fuzzies are music educators. Not all, but some have made great strides in identifying the essence of some goals generally thought to be absolutely and eternally intangible. What follows is an example of what one group did with the goal "be musically creative." I can't tell you what their initial analysis looked like, since I wasn't present when it was completed; but I can show you the first draft of the sentences they wrote to describe their intended performances. Here is the essence of the skills they will expect of their students if they are to be considered musically creative:

Musical Creativity

1. Given the performance of a song by the instructor, improvise an accompaniment on a rhythm instrument.

2. Be able to improvise vocally a harmony part to a well-known song.

3. Be able to play by ear at the keyboard the melody of a given well-known song.

4. Given the performance of a song by the instructor, be able to improvise an accompaniment on a harmonic instrument other than the piano.

5. Given the performance of a song by the instructor, be able to improvise a harmony line on a melodic instrument.

6. Be able to create a melody and notate it. The melody should have a clear climax and a repose (feeling of resolution) at the end.

7. Improvise at the keyboard an accompaniment for a given well-known song.

8. Be able to compose or arrange music suitable for a brief (32 bars or more) dramatic presentation for performance by fellow students.

There it is. There isn't any question whatever about what students will be doing when demonstrating their musical creativity. Others might have different expectations, of course, but that is irrelevant. What matters is that those who want musical creativity have had the courtesy to say what their goal means.

A Case of Therapy

This next example is interesting because of the way the outcome descriptions compared with the goal. While working on the improvement of their curriculum, a nursing faculty decided that one of their goals was that students "be able to develop a therapeutic relationship with adolescents." This is a very "affective" goal, indeed. It was explained that it was extremely important for each nurse to be able to develop such a relationship with adolescent patients, as it contributed significantly to treatment success. Though an important goal, the faculty was not satisfied with their current success in achieving it. There were lectures on psychology and discussions about adolescents, but the number of students the faculty was willing to certify as having achieved the goal was too small to suit them.

Having written the goal, the next step, of course, was to list the performances that represented the goal. But this led to a heated discussion of several topics that appeared to be only peripheral to the main issue. There was talk of patients who were sloppy in their personal habits and of nurses who left patients unnecessarily exposed while dressing or bathing them. There was discussion of several of the problems of being a nurse in this day and age and of the things that happen in hospitals that make their lives dreary or cheery. But there didn't seem to be much discussion of what was meant by "therapeutic relationship." Finally, something happened. One of the faculty members said, with an air of candor, "Look. Nurses aren't supposed to react to patients just because they're different." And within a short time, two statements that described the essence of *their* meaning of "therapeutic relationship" were drafted. They were:

1. Be able to recognize patient characteristics to which the nurse should and should not respond (list of characteristics added).

2. Be able to respond with the proper skill, and withhold response, as indicated by patient characteristics (list of desired skills added).

In plain words, the first of these statements means that when a nurse sees a patient who is dirty or stinky, he or she isn't supposed to say, "Yechhh!" If the patient exhibits offensive or undesirable characteristics, the nurse isn't supposed to look or speak in a derogatory manner. Thus, the first statement describes an ability to recognize *when* to respond and when not to respond. The second statement means that when a nurse sees a patient to whom he or she is supposed to make a response, the nurse has the skill with which to make that response. Note that the first statement is a pure visual-discrimination item that has nothing whatever to do with feeling (affective) and that the second statement describes some sort of cognitive/psychomotor (knowing/doing) skill that again has nothing "affective" about it.

Thus, the essence of a very affective-sounding goal had nothing whatever to do with feeling; nor do the statements describing the meaning of the goal have any affective words in them.

Nor should they. The basis for statements about abstractions such as "therapeutic relationship" is the things people say and the things people do. When we describe those things we want them to say or do to make us willing to label them with the abstraction, there is little need for fuzzies in our descriptions.

There are two other features of this analysis worth noting. The first feature is that what sounded like a vast and profound expectation—"therapeutic relationship"—was ultimately defined by two sentences. Nurses who knew when and when not to respond and who had the skill to respond when appropriate represented the essence of the goal. Period. The second feature is that the analysts discovered that they didn't want nurses to treat adolescents any differently from the way they treated other people. In short, the process of thinking about their expectations caused the analysts to see that this expectation, at least, was inaccurate. The goal analysis caused them to shift their concern from the treatment of adolescents to the broader category of the treatment of patients in general.

With the meaning in hand, it was possible for the faculty to (a) count the number of people who could perform as desired, (b) count the number of instances in which desired performance actually occurred, and (c) decide what to do to get more of what was wanted.

Was this definition of therapeutic relationship "good" or "right"? Doesn't matter, does it? What matters is that this faculty had the courtesy to think deeply about their expectations and to make those expectations public to all those concerned.

Was their definition "humane" or "inhumane"? The procedure for clarifying goals has nothing whatever to do with humanistic or antihumanistic sentiments. To describe the world is not to change it.

To say what one means by a goal is to reduce neither the importance of the goal nor its profundity.

Though the meaning, when seen on paper, may appear trivial—or even *be* trivial—the act of writing it down means merely that what was once secret is now open for inspection and improvement.

An Ounce of Prevention

This last example offers another instance in which the final goal definition was a lot less complex than originally thought. A large oil company asked me to assist with the development of some instruction. "We need our dockworkers to have a proper spill-prevention attitude," said the manager. "We're getting a lot of flak about oil spills, and we want to make sure everyone who handles the oil has a good spill-prevention attitude."

The goal, then, was to "have a proper spill-prevention attitude," and the method of accomplishment envisioned by this manager was "a course." By now, however, you know that it is fruitless to start any action until you know what the action is supposed to accomplish. So, we entered into a discussion (translation: sneaky goal analysis) so that I could find out what they wanted the oil handlers to do. After a while the manager said, "Look, I don't care *what's* going on in their insides; what I want them to do is to follow operating instructions."

"You mean," said I, eagerly pouncing on this specific, "that if they followed operating procedures, you would be willing to say they had the right attitude about spill prevention?"

"I don't *care* about their attitude," he said firmly. "I want them to follow operating procedures."

And that was it. *All* of it. What started out as "have a proper spill-prevention attitude" ended with a single sentence to define it: "Follow operating procedures." Since the operating procedures were all written down, it was easy to tell when they were and were not being followed.

Sometimes it takes many sentences to describe the meaning of a goal; sometimes only one.

Summary

Once the performances representing the essence of the goal are identified, the final steps in the analysis are to draft statements describing each desired outcome and to test those statements with the question, "If these performances are achieved, will I be willing to say the goal is achieved?" When the answer is "yes," the analysis is complete. The complete goal analysis procedure, then, is as follows:

Step One: *Write down the goal in outcome terms.*

Step Two: *Jot down, in words and phrases, the performances that, if observed, would cause you to agree the goal was achieved.*

Step Three: *Sort out the jottings. Delete duplications and unwanted items. Repeat Steps One and Two for any remaining abstractions (fuzzies) considered important.*

Step Four: *Write a complete statement for each performance, describing the nature, quality, or amount you will consider acceptable.*

Step Five: *Test the statements with the question, "If someone achieved or demonstrated each of these performances, would I be willing to say he or she had achieved the goal?" When you can answer "yes," the analysis is finished.*

8

Some Examples

To some people, examples don't examp unless they are set within their own circumstances. This phenomenon, called the not-invented-here factor (or NIH), implies that unless a procedure was invented or developed for a particular area, it couldn't possibly be useful to that area. But fuzzies are fuzzies no matter where you find them, and you can use the same analysis procedure there as well as here. The circumstances might be different, but the procedure is the same.

No Shortage of Fuzzies

A good place to begin is with some examples of fuzzies I've collected over the years. As you read through the list, you will notice that some are more abstract than others, and that some don't seem to make a whole lot of sense. But I assure you that all of these represent examples of goals that someone was, or is, serious about accomplishing.

From the World of Academe

From a junior high school

Develop a favorable attitude toward school

Develop self-actualizing students

Self-concept

Be a self-disciplined person

Self-worth

Develop self-respect

Appreciate democracy

Appreciate American culture

Write legibly

From a high school

Good sport

Music appreciation

Good study habits

Art appreciation

Social adjustment

Self-discipline

Leadership qualities

Likes teacher

Love of learning

Shows initiative

Understands minorities

Enjoys school

Self-respect

Respect for others

Is tolerant

From a dental school

    Professional attitude

    Social consciousness

    Relates basic science to clinical practice

    Graduates with a feeling that the education was relevant

    Has a desire to continue the education

    Has an affection for the university

    Values total patient health

    Thinks like a scientist

    Takes pride in his/her work

From a medical school

    Applies theoretical concepts in practice

    Conducts oneself in a professional manner

    Argues effectively

    Be interested in continuing education

    Establish good rapport with all members of the health team

Communicates effectively

Be a caring physician

Positive self-concept

From a military post-graduate school

Understand the material

Be able to think

Be capable of making original contributions to the field

Be conscious of one's role as manager

Master the fundamentals

No freeloaders

Comprehends the whole picture

Be able to learn on his/her own

Be creative

Develop a proper decision-making attitude

From the World of Work

From an auto manufacturer

Safety conscious

Good diagnostic skills

Handles customer complaints skillfully

Listens to customer complaints

Fixes it the first time

Provides quality service

Sensitive to customer needs

Time efficient

Demonstrates professional attitude

Accepts responsibility

Clearly states customer options

Demonstrates honesty with customers

From a social-welfare department

Ability to accept the client where he/she is

Allows self-determination for the client

Develops good eligibility-worker/client relationship

Be a good eligibility worker

Be an adequate eligibility worker

Know how to close cases

From a supermarket chain

Has pride in work

Customer courtesy

Profit-minded

Friendly

Good front-end service

Clear store

Safe store

Pleasant place to shop

From a marketing division

Cooperative leadership

Cost consciousness

Positive attitude toward the organization

Efficient work organization

Better flow of information

Convince customers

Profit-oriented sales behavior

Good social-political behavior

Knows economic daily news

Knows how to listen

Knows how to judge himself/herself

From a bank

Bank employees will be treated equally in every aspect of employment in order that all employees may achieve maximum use of their abilities.

All employees will perform their daily operations in a manner contributing to responsible corporate conduct.

All employees will act in a socially responsible manner.

From a chemical manufacturer

Communicates well

Good selling skills

Can use a computer

Good leader

Good analytical ability

Good instructor

Is user friendly

No customer complaints

From a boardroom

> Be global minded
>
> Be market sensitive
>
> Think globally, act locally
>
> Develop empowered employees

From politics

> Get the country moving again
>
> Have a balanced budget
>
> Understand the will of the people
>
> Have a "Contract with America"
>
> Be hard on crime
>
> Have a clean campaign
>
> Put America first
>
> Have civil rights

As you read through the above lists, you no doubt noticed some repetition from one domain to another. That's inevitable. Why? Vague terms are interchangeable. For example, what is a "good communicator?" Someone who "listens well." Who has a "professional attitude?" Someone who is a "self-starter" and "takes responsibility." Who takes responsibility? Why, someone with a professional attitude.

The inescapable fact is that there are far fewer things that we want people to do than there are fuzzy ways to describe them.

To verify that for yourself, pick any fuzzy from the preceding pages and see how many other fuzzies you can think of that might have just about the same meaning.

Before moving on, there are a couple of ways to make good use of the above lists. Here's what to do:

1. With a pencil, check the goals that describe process instead of outcome. That is, mark the ones that talk about "developing" or "becoming" rather than "being."

2. Then, re-write the checked items as outcome statements. (This should take only a word or two.)

This is a useful exercise, because you'll never want to begin a goal analysis until the goal is stated as an outcome rather than a process. That way, it is somewhat easier to stay focused on describing what goal accomplishment will look like rather than on the process of getting there.

Sample Goal Analyses

Now that you've seen the range of fuzzies with which people grapple, I'd like to show you some examples of the results of that grappling. The following goal analyses appear in various stages of completion. Though all were alleged to represent the performances that would exemplify a goal (Step 3 of the five-step analysis procedure), you will be able to spot a variety of ways in which they can be improved. As you read through them, see if you can spot:

- "performances" that are still fuzzy,
- statements of process rather than outcome, and
- instances where there is a shift in focus; that is, where one item seems to refer to one group of people and another item refers to another group or to an organization.

Once you've had a chance to review these analyses, you'll be offered a chance to practice improving one or two of them.

Good Physical Appearance

This analysis was conducted by a group of trainers in a police department. Here, they said, is how to recognize someone with good physical appearance:

Always wears clean clothing

Clothing is well-fitting

Wears appropriate hair style (according to regulations)

Has the correct height-weight ratio

Leather and brass are shined

This list may seem short and a bit abrupt, but it is complete in that it describes everything the analyst meant by good physical appearance.

Demonstrates Responsibility

Would this description fit into your own work environment?

Carries out assigned tasks on time

Carries out tasks regardless of the time required

Carries out tasks regardless of whether others have completed their own tasks

Offers solutions to problems outside the immediate job

Plays Well in the Sandbox

This is one of the expressions currently heard around the work environment. "She doesn't play well in the sandbox," or "He doesn't even know his sandbox skills are weak," or "We can't afford to hire anyone who doesn't play well in the sandbox," is how the expression is usually used. But what does that mean? Here are two answers to that question. The first is what it means when talking about kids in a real sandbox; the second is a definition from a real organization:

Kids in a Real Sandbox . . .

share their toys and information

don't hog the good spots in the sandbox

don't section off territory for their own

don't kick sand on other kids

let everyone play

take turns using the toys

bring toys that everyone can use

don't make messes or pollute the sandbox
(you know what that means)

don't pour sand out of the sandbox

People in a Corporate Setting . . .

ask permission before borrowing other people's things

share ideas and information with other people

don't worry about who gets the credit for a good idea

honor written and verbal agreements

share office equipment, supplies, and resources

don't talk behind other people's backs

don't treat other team members like subordinates

don't belittle others or talk down to them

listen to what others have to say

let others have their say without interrupting

are not abrupt, short, or quick with others

are not subservient to the client

are not sarcastic or negative about other individuals, projects, or the organization

provide constructive task-diagnostic feedback to others

provide feedback in an open, timely, candid manner

openly address conflict

respect other people's race, ethnicity, gender, religion

use badges

sign in and out as required

use correct procedure for taking resources off-site

This second list contains quite a few items about which you are likely to ask, "What do they mean by that?"—indicating that the analysis needs work to make the picture of a good sandbox player clear.

Good Tone of Service

Here is an example from a telephone company:

Telephone operators are expected not only to perform their tasks according to company practice and criteria, they are also expected to perform their tasks with "good tone of service." Now the tasks to be performed were well described in a variety of manuals and documents, and there was fairly good agreement about how to tell whether the tasks were being performed properly. Not so with "good tone of service." Because "good tone" is an abstraction (you can't see anyone good toning), twelve supervisors set out to complete a goal analysis.

After several sessions during which many fuzzies were listed and war stories recounted, an interim list of performances was produced:

Actions	**Must Avoid**
acknowledge requests	swearing at customer
express regret	interrupting customer
handle requests promptly	banging*
discriminate between duty	
and beyond the call of duty	
listen attentively	
(criteria: accurate responses, no question repeats)	

Action Should Be Done With:

understandable words	variable pitch
(vocabulary)	calm voice (under stress
accenting of key words	and normal conditions)
proper phrase usage	responses tailored to the
	individual

At this point, the supervisors were ready to move to Step 4 of the analysis procedure and clarify their work further by eliminating duplications and writing each remaining item as

---

*"Banging" means to slam hands, books, or equipment in such a way that the customer detects operator irritation or frustration. Should an operator feel tension to the degree that banging something is the only release, he or she should break the connection before "letting go."

complete sentence. Here is the final result of their delibera-
tions:

Good tone of service

1. Answers with proper phrases within two seconds of
    plug-in.

2. Handles customer requests (i.e., performs operator
    tasks):

without swearing	with words understandable to the customer
interrupting	key words accented
banging	using prescribed phrases
	using variable pitch

3. Demonstrates an ability to listen attentively by respond-
    ing to a series of typical calls (a) accurately and (b) with-
    out asking the customer to repeat the information he or
    she has given.

4. Given the following customer situations (list inserted),
    expresses regret by saying "I'm sorry."

5. Given a series of taped dialogues between operator and
    customer, supervisor is able to identify those calls in
    which the operator responded beyond the call of duty.

When the supervisors were asked if they would agree that
someone had "good tone of service" if he or she did what the
items described (Step 5 of the process), they agreed . . . tenta-
tively. They recognized that there was still a little tidying up to

be done. Even so, they created a basis on which they can make sure that each and every operator performs in accordance with the essence of the goal.

Comment

Notice that this last analysis was conducted as a group activity. Should goal analyses always be done in groups? Absolutely not. The optimum number for an analysis is one or two. If you do it alone, it may take longer to think of all the components of the meaning of the goal than if you have another person available to help trigger your thinking. But every additional person will significantly increase the time it will take to get the job done. There will be war stories to tell, anecdotes about people behavior that need to be recounted, and so on.

Suppose a whole basketful of people will ultimately have to agree on the meaning of a goal. Should they *all* be involved in the analysis? No, not in the original drafting. Go ahead and draft the meaning as best you can, then present your draft to the others (individually if possible). Ask them to modify it to their satisfaction. That will take them a lot less time than if you (a) have a large group of people forging the analysis or (b) ask individuals to write their definitions on a blank piece of paper. The rule is: You'll make more progress if you ask people to fix (edit) something already drafted than if you ask them to create it themselves. Criticizing is always easier than creating.

Here's an example: Suppose you have a meeting with your boss and are told, "I want your team to be more quality conscious when they're working." When you ask for clarification, you're told, "Well, you know, pay attention to quality." On that note, your meeting ends. What to do now? Clearly, you will need to define what "be quality conscious" means before you can take any meaningful action to get more of it. The faster approach would be to do the goal analysis yourself and then ask your team to review and improve your initial draft. You would then have something to take to your boss about which to ask, "If my team did these things, would you agree that they were quality conscious when working?" Your boss will find it a lot easier to suggest changes in an existing list of performances, rather than to try to create a coherent definition of the fuzzy from scratch.

9
A Pinch of Practice

It would be useful to practice the steps of the goal analysis procedure while the steps are still fresh in your mind. So this short chapter will provide some opportunities to do just that.

Practice #1. Write the Goals

Modify the following statements so that each describes an outcome (the end result) rather than a process (how to get to the end result):

Develop a high quality of life.

Improve one's health.

Become an outstanding musician.

Complete training to become a competent engineer.

Learn to be a good citizen.

Develop pride in work.

When you have finished, turn to the next page.

Practice #1 Explanation:

Here's how your goal statements should look:

Develop a high quality of life.

Have a high quality of life.

Improve one's health.

Have good health.

Be healthy.

Become an outstanding musician.

Is (or be) an outstanding musician.

Complete training to become a competent engineer.

Is (or be) a competent engineer.

Learn to be a good citizen.

Is (or be) a good citizen.

Develop pride in work.

Takes pride in work.

Each of these fuzzies now describes the goal in outcome terms rather than in process terms.

Go on to the next page.

Practice #2. Sort a List

Now try sorting a list of performances/fuzzies.

Here is a list of performances from Step 2 of an analysis of the goal, *"takes pride in work."*

<u>Takes pride in work</u>

a. Carries out assigned tasks

b. Likes his/her job

c. Performs tasks well

d. Says favorable things about the job

e. Enjoys his/her work

f. Performs tasks at the level of his/her ability

> Here's what to do:
>
> 1. Cross out duplications;
>
> 2. Place a check mark in front of any item you think is still fuzzy; and then
>
> 3. Write a least one performance that might be useful in defining each fuzzy.
>
> _____
>
> _____
>
> _____
>
> _____

When you've completed the three tasks,
turn to the next page.

Practice #2 Explanation:

Here is the list again for reference:

  a. Carries out assigned tasks

  b. Likes his/her job

  c. Performs tasks well

  d. Says favorable things about the job

  e. Enjoys his/her work

  f. Performs assigned tasks at the level of his/her ability

  1. Cross out duplications.

     Items **b** and **e** seem to be saying the same thing, so either one of them can be deleted.

     Items **a, c,** and **f** all have something to say about carrying out tasks. Item **f** seems to say it best, so I'd delete Items **a** and **c.** That leaves us with:

     d. Says favorable things about the job

     e. Enjoys his/her work

     f. Performs assigned tasks at the level of his/her ability

  2. Put a check mark in front of any remaining fuzzies.

     Item **e** is a fuzzy and should be checked.

  3. Write at least one performance that might be useful in defining each fuzzy.

There are many possibilities here, such as:

- Works longer hours than expected.
- Performs tasks without urging or prompting.
- Explains tasks to others when asked.
- Whistles while working.

What else might employees do to cause you to infer that they enjoy their work?

Go on to the next page.

Practice #3. Complete an Analysis.

Now try to complete a goal analysis that's already been started. For practice, we'll use an example from a previous chapter.

Demonstrates responsibility

a. *Carries out assigned tasks on time*

b. *Carries out tasks regardless of the time required*

c. *Carries out tasks regardless of whether others have completed their own tasks*

d. *Offers solutions to problems outside the immediate job*

Here's what to do:

1. Because goal analysis is useless in the abstract, you will need to select a target for your practice; you will need to say just who is expected to demonstrate accomplishment of the goal. It could be your students, colleagues, administrators, or managers. Whichever target you choose, write the name of that person or group in the space below.

    Target performers: _____

2. Read the goal and list of performances given above. Ask yourself whether you would agree that your target audience could be considered "responsible" if they exhibited the listed performances in the environment in which they work.

3. Delete any items that don't apply.

4. Add whatever performances are needed to cause you to answer "yes" to the question, "If these people did these things, would I consider them responsible people?" (You may need more writing space than is provided below.)

5. Convert each of the performances into sentences that describe the intent as clearly as possible. For example, what does it mean to carry out assigned tasks on time? Does it mean they need to be completed by 8 a.m.? By the time a whistle blows? Before the end of the day?

When you are finished, turn to the next page.

Practice Example #3 Explanation:

It's impossible for me to know which group you targeted for your analysis, of course, so I'll have to select one of my own for the feedback that follows.

The target audience for my analysis is a group of technicians who maintain and repair office equipment. For this group, the goal "demonstrates responsibility" was confined to job performance. Here's how I would re-write the items in complete sentences:

1. **Assigned tasks are completed by established deadlines.**

2. **Tasks are completed regardless of the time required.** (This means that the techs keep working until a task is completed, even if they work past the deadline.)

3. **Assigned tasks are completed regardless of whether others have completed their own tasks.** (This means that "It's not in my job description" is not an acceptable excuse for task incompletion.)

4. **Offers advice to other techs when asked.** (I had to decide what this item meant in terms of my target audience, as the meaning as stated was unclear.)

For the target group I selected, I had to add these items to agree that the techs are performing their work "responsibly."

5. **Keeps tools and test equipment in working order.**

6. **Always keeps a full complement of spare parts at hand.**

7. **Completes the expected paperwork at the completion of each repair or maintenance procedure.**

Your completed analysis will differ from mine, of course,

but your final statements should pass the completion test; the collection of performances should be described in a way that will cause you to agree that the goal would be achieved if someone did what the statements describe.

Tact

With the practice just completed, you should be able to tackle the analysis of almost any goal—when you do it by yourself.

You'll need an additional skill, however, whenever you get other people involved in your goal analyses: Tact. You see, when you ask people what they mean by the abstract words they use, when you ask how they would know one when they saw one, you're treading on tender ground (my wife would call it "thin ice"). It's important, therefore, to approach the analysis with care.

How? Tell yourself that most people aren't used to thinking in terms of specifics. Remind yourself that most people think that being specific about the meaning of a goal somehow makes the goal sound less important, less profound. So give them time to talk their way through the steps. Give them time to change their minds about how they perceive things. Let them make some false starts as they zero in on the meaning of the goal.

Above all, remind yourself that you are likely to be asking people to modify long-held beliefs about the meaning of their cherished fuzzies. So be gentle, and provide some talk-think time. And do a draft analysis by yourself, whenever possible, so that you can give others something to shoot at—give them something to fix, rather than create.

10
Surprise Endings

One thing you learn from repeated use of the goal analysis is that it doesn't always take you where you think you're going. Sometimes, as we have seen in previous examples, it does lead you to the performances that are the meaning of the goal, to the performances that need to be increased or decreased if the goal is to be achieved better. Sometimes, in other words, the analysis takes you through the five steps of the procedure as described (shown below in Figure 1 as Track A).

Sometimes, however, the analysis causes you to shift direction drastically; and sometimes it all evaporates into thin air.

Figure 1

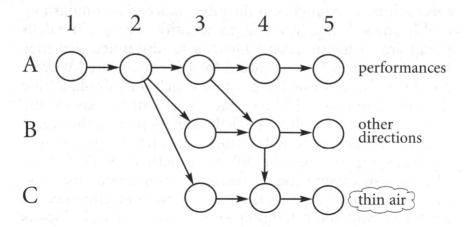

Instead of following Track A, as expected, you may find yourself following Track B or C. This shouldn't be particularly sur-
prising, for it is a common phenomenon in everyone's life. You
may go to the doctor with a firm idea of what is wrong with
you, only to have his or her diagnosis show the problem to be
something entirely different. You may go to the store to buy a
new turn-signal light for your car, and later find that what you
really needed was a fuse. Fixers of electronic devices sometimes find that their "trouble" disappears once someone
remembers to plug in the device. So it goes.

And why not? Nobody's perfect; if we were, there would
probably be no need for analysis procedures, especially the
kind being described in this book. You start off in one direction, and analysis turns you in another. So? That's what analyses are for!

To help prepare you for the various outcomes you will
encounter when analyzing your important goals, I'll provide
some examples that show some of the other-than-as-planned
things that can happen.

From Welfare to Embarrassment

The first example is from the nursing profession, where
there is little question about the importance of accomplishing
health goals. While working to identify the specific skills
important to the practicing nurse, a faculty noted that they
wanted nurses to "show concern for patient welfare." When I
asked them to describe the basis on which they would decide
if someone did indeed "show concern for patient welfare," the
discussion started easily and rolled along merrily. At the beginning, there was a great deal of talk about such things as empa-
thy and sympathy and the difference between these fuzzies.
There was discussion about whether it was necessary for nurses to "really like" their patients if they were to give effective
treatment, and about the problems of working with doctors

and aides. The discussion wasn't exactly pertinent to the problem at hand, but goal analysts learn to allow for some rambling. It seems to help people realize that they normally use quite a few fuzzies during what they consider "technical discussions"; it helps them realize that they don't really know what they are talking about when describing the goals they think important. A little rambling helps clear the air. Asking someone to define a goal in terms of performances *he* or *she* would accept is a little like asking someone to undress in public—if the person hasn't done it before, he or she may need time to get used to the idea.

After ten or fifteen minutes had passed, someone finally said, "Well, no one can be said to exhibit concern for patient welfare if he or she leaves the patient unnecessarily exposed." And the discussion took a sharp turn in a new direction. The participants zeroed in on this topic immediately, and it became clear to those present that concern over "unnecessary exposure" was of more immediate interest than "patient welfare." No doubt items dealing with exposure would be part of what they meant by "patient welfare" (vague terms are interchangeable); but after writing the first item (which was a fuzzy) on their list, they zeroed in on its meaning. Within a minute or two, the faculty had written:

Goal: Shows concern for patient welfare

1. Does not leave patient unnecessarily exposed to:

    fear stimuli

    embarrassment

    treatment

And then, rather than continuing to define this goal, there was strong interest in abandoning it in favor of "unnecessary

exposure to embarrassment." Everyone came up with anecdotes (critical incidents) describing events leading to patient
embarrassment. In each case, the activity or condition leading
to patient embarrassment was jotted down; eventually, the list
looked like this:

Prevents patient embarrassment

1. Controls number of visitors

2. Does *not:*

    a. leave patient exposed physically

    b. treat patient in socially derogatory manner

    c. insult patient's values

    d. insult patient's medical knowledge

    e. bawl out staff in patient's presence

    f. ask more intimate questions than needed to do the job

The remainder of the session was devoted to clarifying the
fuzzies on this list and to testing the list with "the question" to
determine if it represented their meaning of "prevents patient
embarrassment." So, what started out to be an analysis of one
goal (shows concern for patient welfare) ended with the definition of another.

From Listening to Facilitating

This is another example of a change in direction in mid-
analysis. A group of English teachers said that an important
goal in elementary school was to teach kids how to "be better
listeners." When the goal was written on the chalkboard, there
followed a discussion of its importance. After a few minutes, I

reminded the teachers that the next step was to describe what someone might do who represented the goal. But for a time there was only silence.

A lot of thinking . . . but silence.

Finally, one teacher ventured a cautious, "Well, we really can't expect children to listen attentively if they don't have *good hearing.*"

Immediately, somebody wrote "good hearing" on the board.

That prompted another to offer, "And we really can't expect them to listen attentively if it is *too noisy.*"

"Not too noisy" was added to the list.

Then a third said, "Yes, and we really can't expect them to listen attentively unless there is something *worth listening to.*"

"Something worth listening to" was written down. Everyone looked at the board, and then there was a long silence.

And then it seemed as though everyone started talking at once. This happened to be a sharp group of people, and they didn't need any prompting to recognize what had happened. They quickly saw that if they wanted more attention from the kids, they would have to make some changes in their own behavior and in the environment around the kids. A lively discussion followed about just what those changes would be and how they might be put into practice. So, what started out as an intent to decide what to teach children to make them better listeners ended in a description of what the staff would have to do and what the environment would have to be like to make it more likely that students would do what they already knew how to do.

From Responsibility to Effectiveness

Some time ago I had an opportunity to work with the members of a small department charged with improving the "social responsibility of the corporation." These young people had spent a great deal of time trying to decide what the corporation should do to be "more socially responsible," but they succeeded only in pointing fingers and describing what *other* people—government employees, citizens, judge, and vice-presidents—ought to do. The department members were not being deliberately ineffective; they just didn't have a handle on what to do. At this point I was called in to see if I could help. After listening to each member describe his or her under-standing of the mission, it quickly became clear that the group's notion of social responsibility was "what *other* people do." A goal analysis was in order.

This time I decided to involve the entire group of six, as I believed it more important for them to struggle with the process together than to individually critique someone's grand definition of the goal. So we began. "How would you recognize a socially responsible person?" I asked. Clearly, that was the wrong approach. They just couldn't get started. So I tried another tack. "Do you *know* a person you can name whom you would consider socially responsible?"

"Yes," was the immediate reply. "Me!"

Though the comment was made in jest, I took it as a start-ing point and said, "That's a good place to start." With this comment I was signaling that it was OK to horse around with the topic, and that anything they said would be accepted rather than impaled. "What do you do that makes you think of your-self as socially responsible?" I continued, and the discussion blossomed.

"Well, for one thing, I don't steal from the company, like *some* people do."

After writing that comment on a flip chart, I turned to the others and said, "I'm sure you all think of yourselves as social-ly responsible. What do you do that makes you feel that way?" There was quite a bit of response to that, and it seemed as though everyone wanted to talk at once.

"I come to work on time," offered one.

"I give an honest day's work for an honest day's pay," offered another.

"I make suggestions on how things can be improved," offered a third.

"I try to understand the work of people in other parts of the company," offered a fourth.

After a page of such comments was written, someone said, "Wait a minnit. We're not talking about social responsibility; we're talking about an effective employee."

"That's an interesting observation," I replied. "For the moment, though, let's not worry too much about the goal statement. Let's think about what we think we want people to do."

The point of this example is that what started out to be a discussion of what *other* people ought to be like ended with a discussion of what every employee should be like. In effect, the finger that pointed at others slowly turned back toward the pointer.

From Good Judgment to Accurate Decisions

This example was offered to me by a navy lieutenant who worked in one of the many training groups operating within that organization. She described the situation this way:

"We'd been getting a lot of flak from our management about the so-called poor judgments made by the staff of our training department. We were told that we needed to be better at judgment because we were screwing things up for the commanders who put our graduates to work. When we asked what we were doing wrong, however, all we got was a description of the consequences of the errors. Not the mistakes, but the results of the mistakes.

"Finally, we decided to do a goal analysis on good judgment, and it worked out far better than we expected. What we expected was a list of performances that would tell us how to recognize good judgment when we saw it; what we got was a series of flowcharts and checklists showing *exactly* the steps to follow in the performance of good judgment."

She showed me the initial list they drafted, and it looked like this:

Good judgment
- assign criterion levels
- make field/formal decision
- make field-training/formal-training decision

This list made it clear that _in this context,_ good judgment didn't have anything to do with selecting trainees or instructors or with operating ships. It had to do with making decisions related to training. When the analysts completed their Steps Four and Five, their statements looked like this:

1. Given any instructional objective and all available information describing the field situation and trainee quotas, be able to decide whether the objective would best be taught in the field unit or in a formal school environment.

2. For any instructional objective, be able to decide which of five criterion levels should be assigned to it.

(In this example, criterion levels referred to five "levels" of skill, such as "familiarity," "can perform task with supervision," "can perform task without supervision," etc. Each "level" label loosely described the degree of competence required for a given job.)

That was the essence of what they wanted their staff to be able to do regarding good judgment. The interesting thing was that the analysts then moved quickly forward to describing the step-by-step procedure that should be followed when performing each of the above tasks. Figures 2 and 3 show what the flowcharts looked like. You can see how easy it would be to turn the flowcharts into checklists that anyone could follow.

Figure 2

Job: Training Management

Task: Make field-training/formal-training decision

Objective: Given any instructional objective and all available information describing the field situation and trainee quotas, be able to decide whether the objective would best be taught in the field unit or in a formal school environment.

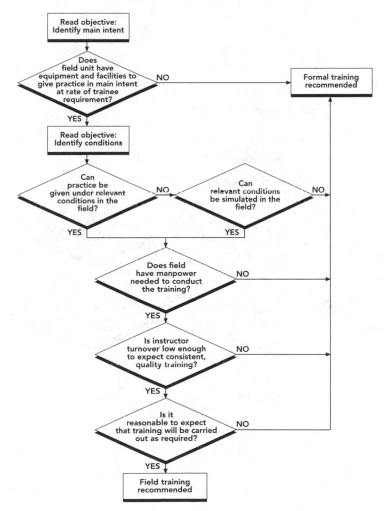

Figure 3

> *Job:* Training Management
>
> *Task:* Set criterion levels
>
> *Objective:* For any instructional objective, be able to decide which of five criterion levels should be assigned to it.

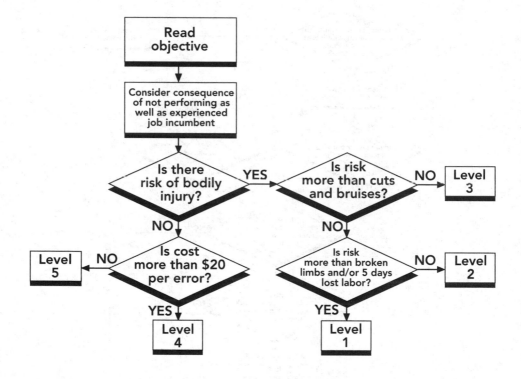

To Thin Air

A few years ago I had a call from a pleasant woman who described a very interesting situation. She said she was a member of a church committee that wanted my help in "establishing an evaluation system by which we can measure the progress of our congregation toward church objectives." Wow! I had never heard of a church that tried to measure the progress of its congregation toward church objectives, and so my ear glued itself to the telephone.

"Do you have any of these objectives written down?" I asked.

"Indeed we do," she replied.

"Would you read me one?" I asked.

"Yes," she said. "Loving service."

Fortunately, I had enough sense to keep my mouth shut while I digested this "objective." Talk about a fuzzy!

Finally, I asked her, "Do you have any more of these—'objectives'—written down?"

"Yes," she replied. "Let me read you the list." And she read:

- loving service
- unselfish devotion
- sincere fairness
- enlightened honesty
- confiding trust
- merciful ministry
- unfailing goodness
- forgiving tolerance
- enduring peace

If you felt a bit overawed while reading that list, I need to remind you that if everyone knew how to be specific about their intentions, they wouldn't need our help. Also, people who have important goals to achieve deserve our best counsel and assistance, regardless of the words they begin with.

I told the woman that there was a series of steps to perform in accomplishing the development of the measurement system the committee was seeking, and that a visit from me wouldn't be profitable until one or two of the steps had already been completed. I explained that she should either work by herself or get her committee together to list the things that people would have to do to be qualified for the labels she listed. We had a long discussion and she took notes to help her memory. She was excited about the activity because she had something very concrete to do.

Alas, when she called back a few weeks later, she sounded defeated. The essence of the problem was that though they talked and talked, no one wanted to talk about specific performances. They wanted to stay at the "merciful ministry" level; they wanted to talk about how to measure *that*, rather than talk about how to measure the *meaning* of that. Too bad, as I was anxious to learn the meaning of those interesting goals.

Summary

Sometimes the goal analysis leads you to a definition of the goal you started with, and sometimes it leads to the definition of another. Sometimes you will be led to give up the analysis in favor of a more urgent activity, and sometimes the content of the analysis will evaporate into thin air. So what? The purpose of an analysis is to give you better information with which to make decisions. If it does that, even by sending you in a different direction, you win!

11
Not for the Casual

This chapter is not for the casual reader or goal setter. It is for those to whom achievement of one goal or another is of the utmost importance or urgency, and who are ready to work toward that end. It is for those who are as interested in accomplishing their goals as they are in defining them.

Additional Steps to Accomplishment

Once you know what successful accomplishment of a goal would look like in terms of what people do, or the results of what people do, you are ready to take some important final steps toward goal achievement. Though these steps are followed *after* a goal analysis is completed, they are included here so that you can see the entire process—from the uttering of a fuzzy that someone says is important to achieve, to accomplishment of that goal.

Step One. *Determine which of the performances revealed by the goal analysis are currently occurring to your satisfaction.* For each of the items on your list of performance statements, determine whether the performance described is already in place. For example, if you want people to show up on time, consult records and people as needed to find out just how many people *do* show up on time; determine the degree to which the actual performance matches the desired perfor-mance. If this performance is already within tolerance, go on to the next item. Should you want people to smile while serv-ing customers, determine whether that is now happening to your satisfaction. If not, mark that item for further action.

Once you have determined what is, and what is not, occur-ring as described by your goal analysis, you are ready for the next step.

Step Two. *Determine which of the non-occurring perfor-mances are due to skill deficiencies and which are due to other causes.* In other words, determine if people aren't per-forming to your satisfaction because they *don't know how,* or for some other reason(s). If they don't know how to perform (or can't perform fast enough or accurately enough or consis-tently enough), it is likely that they will have to be taught how to perform; that is, if there is a skill deficiency, instruction is probably the remedy. The appropriate items on your list can then be turned into instructional objectives,[1] so that relevant instruction can be organized.

On the other hand, if people *do* know how to perform as desired but for some reason are *not* performing, you will need to find out why they aren't doing what they know how to do before you can decide what action to take to increase achieve-ment of your goal. For example, suppose that as a part of what is meant by "good customer service," you expect your bank clerks to smile when serving customers. Suppose further that you determine that only 50 percent of the customers entering your bank are greeted with a smile. What to do? How can you increase the number of smiles?

[1] See *Preparing Instructional Objectives,* Third Edition, R.F. Mager (CEP).

Of *course* people know *how* to smile. Most of them, any-how.[2] If so, why don't they smile as often as expected? To find the answer you will need to carry out a performance analysis[3] that will tell you why people aren't doing what they know how to do and what you can do about it. The performance analysis is likely to reveal that people (a) honestly don't know they are supposed to smile each time they greet a customer; (b) are somehow punished for smiling; or (c) are struggling with an obstacle to desired performance (such as a frantic work load).

At this point you will be ready to take actions that should lead to improved accomplishment of your goal. Arrange for instruction when people don't know *how* to do what they should do, and make the necessary environmental fixes when they're not performing because of other reasons.

Step Three. *If you're really serious about accomplishing your goal, plot your progress on a chart.* And why not? We've seen that an allegedly intangible goal can be defined in terms of the performances that represent it. Since we can tell whether performances occur or don't occur, why can't we plot them on a chart? No reason at all.

And if that goal of yours is as important to achieve as you say it is, then you will surely want to keep track of how you are doing. You will want to compare the steps you take to the results they produce. You may not be able to plot with great precision, and probably wouldn't even want to; but, at the very least, you will want to make sure your actions are taking you in the desired direction.

There is nothing new about the value of indicator charting. Lots of people who care about their effectiveness do it. If you are a manager, you undoubtedly keep tallies and graphs show-ing progress in the events descriptive of company success. If

[2] Some years ago, when a department store chain announced that part of what it meant by "pleasant customer greeting" was that clerks would smile, it was discovered that a small portion of people can't tell when they're smiling in a way that would cause others to agree that they were smiling. The remedy? Have people look into a mirror to see what they look like when asked to smile. A little practice solves the problem.

[3] See *Analyzing Performance Problems,* Third Edition, R.F. Mager and Peter Pipe (CEP).

you are a teacher, you probably keep track of test results and, perhaps, assignment completion and quality. If you are a physician or a nurse, you need no reminders about the importance of charting health (success) indicators. If you are a health-conscious person, you may already be charting your progress in terms of the number of miles walked each day, the number of minutes you exercise, the number of people you can lift above your head, and so on. The only thing that may require a little getting used to is the fact that it is possible to plot the progress of indicators that define some very affective and intangible-sounding states. But it is possible, and it is being done.

A Charting Example:

Let's consider one of the examples used in Chapter 7, that of security consciousness. As you recall, the completed analysis consisted of two performances that indicated an employee's degree of security consciousness.

1. There are no instances in which the person has been found to leave sensitive documents unattended.

2. The filing cabinet is always found locked when it is unattended (when the employee leaves for the day or leaves the room in which the cabinet is located).

Figure 4

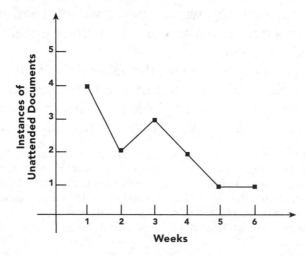

Now then, can you count instances in which sensitive documents have been found unattended? Of course you can. And if you can count them, you can plot them on a graph. In this case, the graph for Susie Schlupopkin might look like Figure 4.

The horizontal line (abscissa) is marked in weeks, and the vertical line (ordinate) is marked in instances. So Figure 4 shows the number of times per week that Susie left sensitive documents unattended. If a weekly count is too insensitive—that is, if it doesn't tell you all you want to know—make a daily count.

As long as the line is moving in the right direction, you can tell yourself that you are moving closer to total achievement of the goal. If it begins to move in the wrong direction, you will need to decide what action to take.

We can plot the second performance of this example in the same way. Here might be the graph of Jeremy Jehumpus:

Figure 5

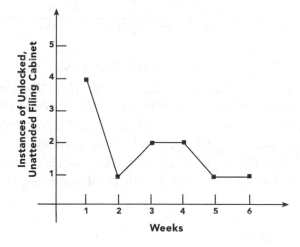

Notice that in Figures 4 and 5, I have plotted instances of *negative* or *un*desired performance. This isn't such a hot idea. You draw attention to whatever you plot, and because attention is highly rewarding, you may get more of the undesired action rather than less. The better approach is to plot the positive whenever you can. Count and plot the number of things that people do right, rather than wrong. In this example, you might plot the number of weeks per month during which there were *no* instances of undesired performance. Better yet, you can plot the percentage of weeks, so that perfect performance will show up as 100% on the graph. Like this:

Figure 6

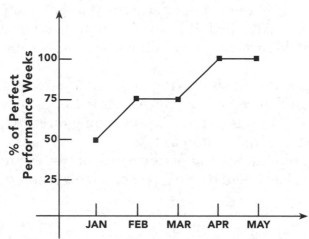

Always accentuate the positive whenever you can. When people find out that you are taking the trouble to plot instances of their performance, you will almost certainly get more of whatever you are plotting. A performance chart is a way of communicating to others the things that are significant to you. When people find out what you consider to be important, you will almost always get more of the performance you want.

Personal Success

More and more people seem to be gearing up to be "more successful" as individuals. They are acting to "take charge of their lives," as the slogan says. "Improve personal success" and "take charge of my life" are fuzzies, of course; so how do these people proceed? What do they do to get more of what they want? By now you know the answer.

First they do what amounts to a goal analysis, to determine just what success would look like if they had it. Then they pick an easy performance to work on, plot how they are doing *now*, and keep track of their progress.

A separate analysis is done in each of the areas (social, family, financial, professional, health, and so on) in which increased success is desired. This method is easier than trying to deal with "personal success" in a single lump. When completing each analysis, it is important to remember that what is important to you is what matters, rather than what the neighbors say or what television projects as important; and it is important to remember that little things count.

I have a friend who constantly tries to improve himself by this method. When he first did a goal analysis, he discovered that the control of his own time was important to him. He hadn't realized it before, but a large portion of his time was controlled by others who came into his office for a variety of reasons—or for no reason at all. Once he learned that time control was important, he decided to find out just how much of his time was currently other-directed. He set up a recorder in his office, and whenever he changed activity, he would say something into the recorder, such as "10:15 Charlie came in to chat," or "10:30 Left for meeting called by boss."

After a month he discovered two things: First, about 60 percent of his time was taken up by things that other people wanted him to do; and second, as soon as people learned he was keeping track of his time, they reduced their demands on his time. They would think twice, for example, before entering his office just to pass the time of day, because they knew this activity would lead to an entry such as "2:45 Mary came in to shoot the breeze."

His plot for this initial analysis looked something like this:

Figure 7

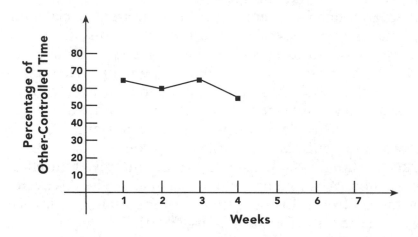

Now that my friend knew how well he was doing in regard to time control, the next thing he had to decide was how well he would have to do to consider himself successful.

Zone of Reason

We are now at a point where the zone of reason becomes a useful tool. After all, *perfection* is seldom a reasonable expectation. But if perfection is unreasonable, what *is* reasonable? The answer to that will always depend on your knowledge of the situation and on the strength of your desire. Consider Figure 7. Would it be reasonable to suppose that anyone can control *all* of his or her time—that is, would it be reasonable to expect *not* to have to spend *any* time doing things that others wanted you to do, or doing things you would rather not do (such as taking out the garbage, writing reports, keeping tax records)? If total time control isn't a reasonable expectation, what is? Ten percent? Forty percent?

How important is it to achieve the goal? How much control can you exert without jeopardizing your job or your friendships? You have to decide what is reasonable. After reviewing his situation, my friend decided that since he was in a business that required a fair number of meetings and conferences, a 40/60 split was a reasonable expectation; that is, if he could reduce the percentage of his time that was other-directed to 40 percent from 60 percent, he would consider that success. So he drew a line across his chart at 40 percent (Figure 8). Any time the plot line dipped to 40 percent or below, he would tell himself he was successful. He wouldn't wait until the line reached zero, since that was unreasonable. The zone of reason was anywhere from zero to 40 percent.

Figure 8

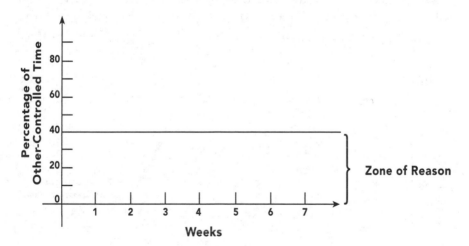

In effect, the line you draw indicates the target you have decided is reasonable to achieve. It is your criterion of success for the item being plotted. Any time your plot line touches or passes that target line, you can tell yourself that you are successful (which is pretty heady stuff).

You might set your zone at different positions at different times. You might begin by noting what you get now in the way of the desired performance and then decide you will determine that your goal for the year is reached if you achieve a five percent increase. You would thus set your zone between five percent above current performance and 100 percent performance. Anything above five percent improvement is considered success and will cause you to agree your goal is achieved, at least so far as that performance is concerned.

In some instances, your zone may be formed not by a horizontal line across the graph, but by a line that angles upward from the origin (the point at which the horizontal and vertical axes meet). Points plotted above that line would fit into your zone of reason; those plotted below the line would not. For example, as I sit here squeezing out one sentence at a time, I look at a chart on the wall before me (Figure 9). This chart plots the number of pages that I produce each day. As my objective is a daily output of at least four pages, I've drawn a

Figure 9

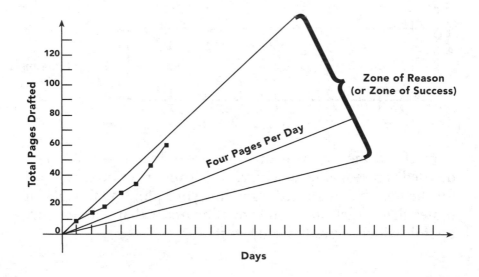

line showing that expectation. That's my zone of reason. I know from experience that with effort I *can* produce four pages per day, and I know I *must* produce that much or more if I am to finish anything within the next century. The chart is useful as a reminder to keep working until I can record progress somewhere within the zone of reason (anywhere on or above the line).

When managing a self-paced course in which students are encouraged to move at their own rates, one finds that some students progress faster than others. But sometimes the slower student is slower because he or she is more thorough and more interested in the course rather than because the student is less capable. Figure 10 shows the progress of three hypothetical students through such a self-paced course. Once experience has been gained with actual students, it is easily possible to set the lower limits of the rate at which the students must progress if they are to complete the course within the time allotted. (Occasionally, there is reason to set an upper limit as well.)

Figure 10

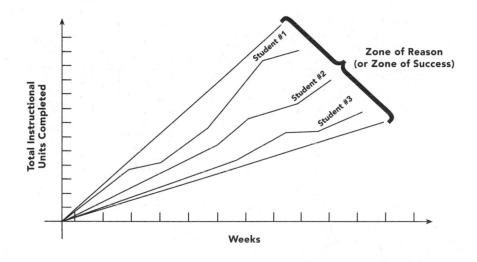

Figure 11 is the Progress Chart used in a two-week performance-based, self-paced workshop called Criterion-Referenced Instruction.[4] The graph line shows the cumulative number of modules (units of instruction) students must complete each day if they are to finish the course in the time allotted. If they have completed at least enough modules to match or exceed the line, they can tell themselves that they will have adequate time to complete the entire course by the time allotted. This line tells students precisely what is meant by "successful completion" of the course.

Figure 11

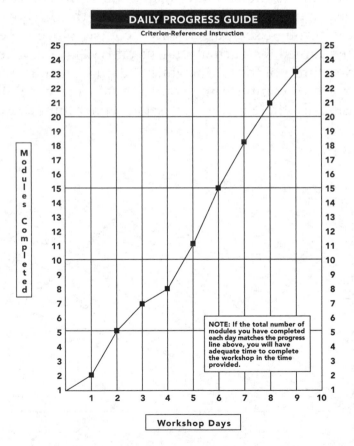

[4] *CRI (Criterion-Referenced Instruction): Practical Skills for Design Instruction that Works,* Fourth Edition, The Center for Effective Performance, Atlanta, GA, 1994.

The Unchartables

Suppose you set out to plot the performances that define your goal and find it difficult to collect the information you want. Suppose it turns out to be impractical to determine whether the performances you are interested in actually are occurring. Then what? Well, one of two things.

If you cannot collect the information you need to plot the performances, you have reason to wonder whether the performances are a reasonable meaning of your goal. If, for example, you define good citizenship in terms of what you expect a person to do ten years hence, you will find it impossible to find out whether you are at all successful in achieving that goal. Sure, you want your employees to vote in every national election, but there is no practical way you can find out if they do. So, wonder if that is a reasonable expectation.

If you conclude that your definition is reasonable but that there is no easy way to collect information to plot . . . for now, that's OK. Nobody said that all fuzzies are easy to define (try a goal analysis of "reverence," for example). If you can't tell how you are progressing, you can't tell. Just make sure you refrain from labeling people as either representing or not representing your goal if you can't tell whether they are performing as you want.

For example, if part of what you mean by "loyalty" is "doesn't badmouth the company," and you can't tell the difference between badmouthing and constructive criticism, just hold off with the snap judgments about who is loyal and who is not. If you have no accurate way to find out what people are saying, or if you decide it would be unethical even to try, either change your expectations or refrain from making inferences about who is and who isn't a goal achiever. But above all, try to remember that it is a highly questionable practice to label someone as having achieved or not achieved a goal state when you don't even know what you would take as evidence of achievement. That is almost as reprehensible as grading students on their "attitudes" when the basis for that grading is unknown and when the basis for the judgment shifts from one student to another.

Mapples and Moranges

Which brings us to a final point. Suppose you are charting two or more performances that collectively define some sort of attitude. It could be that you're charting the components of "favorable attitude toward customers." You have a separate graph for each performance and regularly put a dot on each to show progress.

Now then, if you are charting the performances that are the meaning of your attitude goal, aren't you plotting the attitude? Of course you aren't plotting the attitude directly, as there is no way to get a dipstick into wherever the attitude "is" for a direct reading—by definition. You can, however, plot the basis for your statements and judgments about attitudes; and that is just about as good. Better, in fact, since you can make adjustments as your meaning becomes more sophisticated simply by changing one or more of the charts. Does it matter whether you are *really* plotting an attitude? Isn't taking steps to see if you are moving in the desired direction the real thing that matters (Answer "yes" or "yes")?

Perhaps you are thinking that the indications from each of the charts should be *combined* into a single indicator, and that *that* could be called the attitude chart, if anything is. Perhaps. It is certainly a tempting thought. But if you try it, you are sure to be harassed, bludgeoned, and boiled in oil by the statisticians who understand such things. For one thing, it would be like adding apples and oranges, except worse. You can say that if you have three apples and four oranges, you have seven fruits. But what have you got when you add three apples and four maps? Seven mapples? Seven something, surely; but it just isn't meaningful addition.

There is another problem with combining the content of the various charts into a single number: Most of the charts you want to combine are likely to have intervals of different sizes.

So if you combine your numbers into some sort of total success indicator, you will never know exactly what those numbers mean. But wait a minute. What's the difference? What if a total number has no statistical validity? As long as it makes you feel good to know that you are getting closer to goal achievement, isn't that enough? Well, yes and no. It's enough if you are the only one who sees the numbers and you are *not making judgments about other people* based on those numbers. Otherwise, do not try to combine your charts. Decide what is a reasonable expectation for each performance, mark in the zone of reason on each chart, and concentrate on improving the individual performances. Once you have designated the performances that are important, you can forget about the goal statement that was useful only in getting you started.

12
Let's Pretend

Rather than finish things off with a dreary summary that might send you away with your attitude all wrinkled up, you might find it more useful to check out your ability to explain the topics presented in this book.

Let's pretend you are talking with someone who knows you have just finished reading this book. This person is mildly curious but doesn't know the territory. He or she is the Fuzzy-minded type, whose vague feeling is that only intangibles have "real" value and that anything specific or measurable is automatically base or trivial. He or she seems to believe that those things that are impossible or difficult to understand are somehow profound and that those things that are clear or simple cannot possibly be worthy of his or her respect.

I'll provide his or her side of the interview, and you provide the replies. Afterward, you can compare your sharp and pungent explanations with mine.

Turn to the next page.

Inquirer: Goal analysis, huh? What's that? Do you know enough about it to describe it in a sentence or two?

You:

Inquirer: Why in the world would you want to do a goal analysis?

You:

Inquirer: But how would I know when I should do a goal analysis?

You:

Inquirer: How would I know one of these broad statements of intent when I saw one?

You:

Inquirer: Can you briefly describe the steps in doing a goal
                   analysis?

You:

Inquirer: What will I be able to do when the analysis is
                finished?

You:

Inquirer: Well, maybe *your* subject is trivial enough to be
                reduced to a bunch of little performances, but
                mine is intangible.

You:

Inquirer: Oh, yeah? Well, let me tell you something. My goals can't be chopped up into little pieces. Besides, you don't think it's necessary to analyze *every* goal to its last ounce of meaning, do you?

You: (Steady now.)

Inquirer: HMMMmmmmmmmmmmm . . .

If you'd like to compare your responses with the sort of thing I might say, look at page 147. You might also want to check your accuracy by reviewing the text.

Inquirer: *Goal analysis, huh? What's that? Do you know enough about it to describe it in a sentence or two?*

Me: Sure. Goal analysis is a procedure for helping to define broad goals to the point where their main elements (performances) are described. It is a way to discover the essence of what a goal means.

Inquirer: *Why in the world would you want to do a goal analysis?*

Me: Some goals are quite important to achieve. The goal analysis will help you describe what you mean by success, help you to recognize achievement when you see it. If you know what it is you want to achieve and know what achievement looks like when you have it, you can make better decisions about how to get there.

Inquirer: *But how would I know when I should do a goal analysis?*

Me: Whenever you have a broad statement of intent that is important to do something about.

Inquirer: *How would I know one of these broad statements of intent when I saw one?*

Me: Easy. A broad statement describes an abstraction, such as "understand," "develop," "know," "internalize," or "appreciate." If the statement doesn't answer for itself the question, "How would you recognize one when you saw one?" It's a goal ripe for analysis.

Inquirer: *Can you briefly describe the steps in doing a goal analysis?*

Me: *First,* write down the goal (Step One).

               Second, jot down the performances that define the goal (Step Two). Do that by answering whichever of these questions seems more relevant or comfortable to you:

               a. What would a person be doing that would cause me to say he or she had achieved the goal?

               b. Given a room full of people, what is the basis on which I would separate them into two piles—those who had achieved the goal and those who had not?

               c. How would I recognize the goal achievement when I saw it?

               d. Thinking of someone who does represent the goal, what does he or she do or say that makes me willing to say so?

               Third, go back over the list and tidy it up (Step Three). Cross out duplications and items that, on second thought, don't describe what you want to say. Carry out Steps One and Two for any remaining fuzzies.

               Fourth, describe each important performance in a statement (complete sentence) that identifies the manner or extent (or both) of the performance you require to be satisfied the goal is achieved to your liking (Step Four).

Finally, modify these statements until you can answer "yes" to this question: "If someone achieved according to these statements, would I bc willing to say he or she had achieved the goal?" (Step Five). Collectively, these statements will represent the meaning of the goal.

Inquirer: *What will I be able to do when the analysis is finished?*

Me: You can do a number of things. You can take steps to find out how things are now going in regard to the performances you want; you can take steps to get more or less of each of the desired performances separately; and you can chart your progress.

Inquirer: *Well, maybe your subject is trivial enough to be reduced to a bunch of little performances, but mine is intangible.*

Me: Perhaps you're right. And if so, it means there is no way to tell whether you are achieving your goals. Therefore, you mustn't claim you are doing so. Unless you perform a goal analysis on your intangibles, you will never know which of them can be achieved, nor by what means.

Inquirer: *Oh, yeah? Well let me ask you something. You don't
                think it's necessary to analyze every goal to its last
                ounce of meaning, do you?*

Me: No. Only those goals that are important to
                achieve. *You don't change the world by describing
                it, but you put yourself in a better position to move
                things in your direction if you know what that
                direction is. So, goal analysis is not for every goal.
                Only for those that are important to achieve.*

Inquirer: HMMMmmmmmmmmmm.

BOOK FIXERS EXPOSED!

PRESS RELEASE   **For release upon receipt**

At a hastily called press conference attended by two editors and a clerk-typist, Robert Mager, maker of miniMager-manuscripts, ripped the lid off the secrecy surrounding the development of his three editions of *Goal Analysis*. Not only did he name names, but he identified just who was associated with each phase of manuscript testing. Those present gasped at the revelations.

When asked whether their contributions weren't extremely useful in improving the manuscript, Mager grudgingly replied, "Oh, sure. If it weren't for them, the whole thing would be a shambles. They made me throw out exampless examples and not-so-funny funnies; they choked on things that turned them off and gagged at explanations that didn't explain. Instead of finding a wall to spray on, they scribbled all over my pages with suggestions for improvement and ideas for alternatives. But it all came down to the same thing: Work, work, work!"

"Do you think there is something to be gained from exposing these kindly souls to public glare?" he was asked.

"You bet I do," he replied energetically. "Once they are known, they'll get what's coming to them."

Mager then read the names of those who contributed so graciously to the tryouts, accompanied by blaring trumpets and crashing cymbals. "But I'm not done yet," Mager stammered as someone tried to lead him from the stage. "I'm going to print all their names for the amazement and admiration of the reading public, for Posterity—that's just a few miles from Retrospect, you know—and for raucous cheering by all."

And so it was.

Book Fixers Exposed!

First and Second Editions

1. **Continuity check** (does everything hang together?): David Cram, John Warriner.

2. **Content check** (does it do what it is supposed to do?): Margo Hicks, Ed Krenz, Sue Markle, Sarah Morris, Maryjane Rees, Andy Stevens, Phil Tiemann.

3. **Attitude check** (does it contain unnecessary turnoffs?): Dorothy Carver, Jim Hessler, Bill Hicks, Dan Kratocvil, Frank Moakley, Vernon Rees, Charles Selden, Nancy Selden, Walt Thorne, Jack Vaughn, George Whiting.

4. **Word check** (are there obscure words that can be traded in for common ones?): Brad Mager, Randy Mager.

5. **Cover check** (is the cover design responded to favorably?): Vince Campbell, Jerry Harrison, Jeanne Mager, Debbie Michaels, Sarah Morris, Dick Niedrich, Laura Newmark, Peter Pipe, Oscar Roberts, Bud Robertson, Bill Shanner, Jim Shearer.

Third Edition

Another batch of graffitists contributed to the shaping of the present edition.

Good and bad samples from their goal analysis collections were generously offered by Dan Raymond and Bonnie Abney.

Initial trampling was kindly undertaken by that virtuoso manuscript bashist, David Cram. Once the reeling manuscript was resuscitated, another group of miscreants gleefully added their footprints: Marianne Hoffman, Kay Newell, Dan Lansell, Verne Niner, and Eileen Mager.

Index

Practice
in completing a goal analysis,
108–111
in delivering customer service,
126–127
in explaining goal analysis,
141–150
in goal writing, 103–104
in recognizing "fuzzy" goals,
24–31
in sorting performances, 105–107
Prediction statements, 17–18
*Preparing Instructional Objectives
(Mager)*, 126
Pride in work
performance criteria for, 105–107
performance identification for,
56–57
Problem description checklist, 71
Process, versus outcome, 44, 46, 66,
95, 103–104
Production engineers, goal analysis
by, 13
Professionalism, improving, 1
Progress charts, 127–130
for self-paced courses, 135–136
Punctuality, performance criteria for
demonstrating, 67
Punishment, of favorable
performances, 58, 62
Purposeful activity, 3

Quality consciousness, goal
analysis for, 101–102
Quality engineers, goal analysis by,
13

Rambling, during goal analysis,
115
Recognizing, as a covert
performance, 38
Religious objectives, goal analysis for,
123–124

Reporting, performance criteria for,
69–72, 73–74
Responsibility
performance criteria for
demonstrating, 68, 96, 108, 110
social, 117–119
Results. See also Outcomes
of goal analysis, 113–114
plotting on a chart, 127–128
relationship to actions, 3
versus process, 44
Rewards, positive, 129–130

Safety consciousness,
performances associated with,
54–56
Sales managers, goal analysis by, 13
Security consciousness
charting, 128–130
performance criteria for, 77–78
Self-concept, improving, 1
Self-paced courses, 135–136
Service industries, performance
criteria for, 98–102
Sharing, as a performance criterion,
97, 98
Significant incident analysis, 9
Skill deficiencies, 126–127
Skill level, assessing, 74
Skills
improving, 23
making judgments about, 50
Social development, performance
criteria for, 97–98
Social responsibility, improving,
117–119
Specifics, thinking in terms of, 111
Statements, "Hey, Dad" Test for,
34–35
Student progress, charting, 135–136
Subject areas, topics worth teaching
in, 80
Success. See also Personal success

MORE GREAT BOOKS FROM DR. ROBERT F. MAGER!

Dr. Robert F. Mager has authored one of the most extensive and renowned collections of books and resources on issues of human performance in existence today. These books are considered to be *the* reference library for anyone serious about educating others and improving human performance. You'll find everything you need to learn how to:

- develop successful instruction,
- find realistic solutions to performance problems,
- measure the results of your instruction,
- generate positive attitudes in learners,
- and much more!

Order your copies today and get resources you'll use for a lifetime.

	Quantity	x Price=	Total
Measuring Instructional Results *How to determine whether your instructional results have been achieved*		x $23.95=	
Preparing Instructional Objectives *A critical tool in the development of effective instruction*		x $22.95=	
How to Turn Learners On… without turning them off *Ways to ignite interest in learning*		x $22.95=	
Analyzing Performance Problems *How to figure out why people aren't doing what they should be, and what to do about it*		x $23.95=	
Making Instruction Work *A step-by-step guide to designing and developing instruction that works*		x $24.95=	
Goal Analysis *How to clarify your goals so you can actually achieve them*		x $22.95=	
The How to Write a Book Book		x $17.95=	
Troubleshooting the Troubleshooting Course		x $22.95=	
What Every Manager Should Know About Training		x $22.95=	
Subtotal			
Shipping & Handling*			
GA residents add 7% sales tax to the subtotal plus shipping and handling			
Total Order			

* Please add $6.00 for the first book, plus $1.50 for each additional book. Please allow four weeks for delivery by UPS Ground Service.

Name _____

Phone _____ Fax _____

Organization _____

Address _____

City _____ State _____ Zip _____

☐ My check or money order for $_____ is enclosed

Charge my ☐ Visa ☐ Mastercard ☐ AmEx   Exp. Date _____

Card Number _____

Name on Card _____

Please send this form and your check, money order, or credit card number to:

CEP
P.O. Box 102462
Atlanta, GA 30368-2462

Call 1-800-558-4CEP for volume discount information.

Call for shipping charges on international orders.

For credit card orders, fax this order for faster delivery: (770) 458-9109 or use our website at: www.cepworldwide.com